Acclaim for Margit R. Crane's
HOW TO TRAIN YOUR PARENTS IN 6½ DAYS

"What an amazing and insightful book! As a teacher of teens and a mother of teenagers, this book helped me to realize how much I still have to learn. Margit Crane speaks directly to teens, in an authentic, compassionate and witty way, addressing key issues that can transform any teen-adult relationship. *How to Train Your Parents* is an awesome tool (maybe even a secret weapon) for teenagers, helping them to see their own power."
--Dr. Betina Hsieh, Secondary Education, Berkeley, California

"Margit Crane's many years of experience brilliantly shine through in this extraordinary book designed to bridge the gap between teens and their parents. As a teacher, I appreciate that Margit incorporated all the elements necessary to reach her teenage audience including: language that they can relate to, simple steps to follow, personal experience, humor, and encouragement. And parents can use *How to Train Your Parents'* strategies to enhance their relationship with children of all ages." –Lynn Angalet, M.Ed., Tween Educator

"How to Train Your Parents in 6½ Days is a stroke of genius! It's written in language that is accessible and engaging to teens. It's also full of insights into a teen's mind for parents and other adults – counselors, teachers, advisors, leaders, and coaches – who work with teens but have forgotten what it's like to be one."
–Rabbi Justin Kerber, Temple Emanuel, St. Louis, Missouri

"As a pastor, uncle, and new foster dad I know that I get it wrong with the kids in my life all the time. Margit gets how adults' quirks and obsessions get in the way of connecting with teens. This book will grab teens and their parents and help them not only understand each other, but enjoy each other more." –Rev. Peter Ilgenfritz, U.C.C., Seattle

"Are your parents driving you crazy? Are you driving your parents crazy? *How to Train Your Parents in 6½ Days* will make all the craziness go away and quickly! Margit Crane's humor, smarts, and help come shining through as she leads you, day-by-day, to a place of understanding, calm, and respect. Your parents will respect you, listen to you, and actually behave better!" –Amy Lang, 3-time Moms Choice Award® Winner, National Speaker, and Creator of Bird + Bees + Kids®

"Margit Crane definitely knows teenagers. *How to Train Your Parents in 6½ Days* is the perfect solution if your folks are driving you nuts. If you're tired of arguing with your parents or step-parents, or they just don't get you, this is the book for you. This stuff will definitely work with teachers and bosses, too!
- Christian Zsilavetz, High School Educator

"How to Train Your Parents in 6½ Days encourages teens to think about their parents in a different light and, surprisingly, will encourage parents to examine their relationship with their own parents as well as with their teens. Parents: if you want to improve your communications with your teen and, ultimately, set a life-long pattern, buy this book!" –Roberta, Parent of Daryn (below)

"I loooooooove this book! It's so good, so funny, and oh so helpful. If you want to build a better relationship with your parents, Margit Crane's book is the best one on the market. She is able to put you in your parents' shoes and put them in yours. The writing style in the book is hilarious and communicates the pointers and tips very well to teens. When you finish reading this book, you will be able to get your parents to treat you the way you want to be treated."
–Daryn, age 14, Daughter of Roberta (above)

"Hi, I'm 'Nate' from the book. Margit is great and a good friend to us kids and the things she says in her book really work. My parents learned everything isn't my fault and I learned the way parents think about things and I have more confidence."
–Nate, age 11½

"After reading *How To Train Your Parents,* I now understand what it's like to be a parent. I loved the activities that you can do in the book. This is a book that both teens and parents will find fun."
-Arden, age 12

"This is a great book! I enjoyed how easy it was to understand and how many great tips it gave me. It even taught me to deal with any upcoming problems."
-Caroline, age 14

"I've stopped trying to win and I learned I was hurting myself. I listen to my parents more and things are much calmer. My parents give me more privileges, which is sweet. Excellent book."
-Ethan, age 16

"Before, I got angry at my parents a lot and they got angry at me too. It seemed like they were trying to trap me. Now it's much better. Anyone can use a microscopic part of this book and get more respect."
–Stella, age 17

MARGIT R. CRANE

HOW TO TRAIN YOUR PARENTS IN 6½ DAYS

a teen's guide to raising people you can live with

By

Margit R. Crane

If you are unable to order this book from your local bookseller, you may order from Amazon.com, CreateSpace.com, or from HowToTrainYourParents.com

The techniques described and the advice given in this book represent the opinions of the author, based on her experiences. The author is not licensed to practice medicine and, therefore, expressly disclaims any responsibility for any liability, loss, or risk, personal or otherwise, which is incurred as a result of using any of the techniques or recommendations suggested herein. If in any doubt, or if requiring medical advice, please contact the appropriate health professional.

ISBN-10: 1466280727
ISBN-13: 978-1466280724

Printed in the U.S.A.

DEDICATION

To all my students and clients:
You have given my world so much

* SPARKLE & JOY *

♥ Thank you for sharing your lives with me ♥.

CONTENTS

"Because of their size,
parents may be difficult
to discipline properly."

-- P.J. O'Rourke

INTRODUCTION

---

1. How often do your parents nag you?
   - ☐ Rarely
   - ☐ Weekly
   - ☐ Daily

2. What do they nag you about the most?
   - ☐ Schoolwork
   - ☐ My attitude
   - ☐ Other stuff

3. How would it feel to have them *stop* nagging and yelling?
   - ☐ What a relief!
   - ☐ I'd wonder if they were sick
   - ☐ Is that possible?

Let's cut to the chase. I'm not going to waste your time.

Here's all you need to know before you get started working with the material in this book:

- ✓ Yes, it's possible to get your parents to stop yelling and nagging

- ✓ No, you don't have to take 6½ days for it to work. You can take 5½ days, 12½ days or 7¾ weeks. It'll still work.

- ✓ No, it won't work without some effort on your part.

- ✓ Yes, you can have a bad attitude about the whole thing and think this is stupid, and it will still work, at least up to the part about pretending to have a good attitude. At that point, you've got to pretend to have a good attitude.

✓ Yes, you can e-mail me (Margit@MargitCrane.com) if you have questions, concerns, or good things to tell me, like: "Hey Margit! I read your book and I think you're the smartest adult in the world." I guarantee that will get my attention. ☺

✓ Absolutely! Show this to your parents, if you want. Many parents work on this with their kids. In fact, you may want to buy an extra copy for them.

Or, you may each want to purchase a journal to write about some of the things you're discovering. That way, you can keep your thoughts private if you want.

Or, there are pages in the back of the book you can use to take notes or draw or create your plan for World Peace or whatever.

Want more details? Keep reading.

WHAT YOU CAN EXPECT FROM READING THIS BOOK

Let's start backward. Let's start with the results. Here are the results you can expect from reading this book and doing the oh-so-simple exercises.

You will learn:
- ✓ What bugs parents the most
- ✓ Why parents are so overprotective
- ✓ Why they seem not to trust you
- ✓ Why they get so angry/frustrated/confused
- ✓ Why they seem to have a never-ending need to embarrass you

You will be able to get your parents to:
- ✓ Accept your feelings
- ✓ Listen to your ideas
- ✓ Trust you more
- ✓ Give you more freedom
- ✓ Agree with you

You will experience:
- ✓ Fewer arguments
- ✓ More respect for who you are and what you can do
- ✓ Better relationships, with friends, parents, and teachers
- ✓ Better grades (really!)
- ✓ More say in family decisions

And you will feel:
- ✓ Smart!
- ✓ Confident!
- ✓ Powerful!
- ✓ Free!
- ✓ Happy!
- ✓ And, *maybe,* more Attractive!

CHECK OUT THE CHAPTER TITLES

DAY ONE – *"What's Wrong With Them? Parents Behaving Badly."* How do your parents connect with you (or disconnect from you)?

DAY TWO – *"Parental Paranoia: It's What's For Breakfast."* Believe it or not, parenting is scary! Time to learn why.

DAY THREE – *"Can You See Me Now? Teens, Parents, and Stereotypes."* Lazy, goofball, gangster . . . We look at what's wrong with the way adults view teens.

DAY FOUR – *"You're in Charge. Be the Change."* A good trainer knows how to inspire his trainee. Do you?

½ DAY – *"Excuses, Excuses."* What do you do when you don't want to do anything at all?

DAY FIVE – *"Eyeball Overhaul: Change Your View, Change Your Experience."* We're going to shake you up and break down all the assumptions you have about your parents.

DAY SIX – *"No More Power Struggles: You Talk, Your Parents Listen!"* You'll learn how to get your point across without ticking off your parents.

MAKE YOUR "TRAINING" STRONGER

Periodically, you'll see a "Thought Bubble," like the one just to the right. These represent **key ideas** that are worth your time and thought.

> Easy exercises can still be super powerful.

Plus, throughout each day, there will be some fun exercises. These aren't tests. There are no wrong answers. I'm going to be throwing quite a bit of new information at you and it's always good to take some time to play with new ideas so you can make them your own.

Some of the exercises will be *so* easy you just might think they're too stupid to bother with. Don't let their simplicity fool you – these are super powerful. They will help you better understand yourselves and your parents, and with that understanding – *whoa baby!* – You will be able to radically change your relationship and train your parent fast!

Are you feeling a bit fearful about the exercises?
Feeling resentful that your parents bought this book for you?

I get afraid and angry as well, even though I'm an adult.

One thing I do when I'm starting something new or when I have to do something I don't want to do is to list what my thoughts are about the situation.

What are my fears?
Why am I so angry?

Now, I know you can do this in your head, but did you know that as long as your thoughts, concerns, and/or fears stay in your head they can't get resolved?

Don't believe me?
I didn't either the first time I heard this. But it's true.

In fact, *the* Albert Einstein once said:

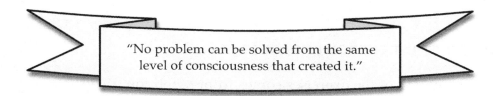

"No problem can be solved from the same
level of consciousness that created it."

Put into simpler English, *this statement means we can't change our negative thoughts or solve our problems by ourselves.* We need to get them out of our heads and share them. And a first step can be writing them down on paper.

Imagine you're a little kid sitting in a mud puddle and you're trying to make a castle or build a mountain. The mud is wet, slippery and, well, muddy. In order to actually build, you need something dry and solid to build on. As long as you're in the mud, working with mud, the thing you want to make can't actually be made.

It's like this in your brain.
You have a great idea, or a negative thought, or a big fear, or a brilliant plan but as long as it's sitting in your brain it can't really become anything except what it started as. It will still be "mud."

Figuring things out by yourself doesn't work that well, surprisingly.

For a great idea, a negative thought, or a brilliant plan to become something else, it needs a new environment. It needs to exit your brain. And writing your fears down on paper is a great way to give your fear or anger a new environment.

What thoughts do you have about starting to work through this book? I'll start; you can write down some of your own thoughts.

✓ It's a trick. I'm just being brainwashed!

✓ It won't work. I'll put out all this effort for nothing.

✓ _____

✓ _____

✓ _____

The more you're willing to share your thoughts here, the quicker you'll progress.

PRACTICE THESE EXERCISES REGULARLY

The power of the exercises comes from repetition. Keep repeating these activities. *It can take up to 90 days to change a habit,* so don't stop just because you finished one day's assignments and it's a new day of training.

Keep the momentum going! You're going to become a lean, mean parent-training machine, and you will need to "keep in shape" just like athletes or musicians or artists keep their skills up.

DO YOU HAVE TO DO ALL THE EXERCISES?

Well no, but if you're just dreaming small, how fun is that? Sure, you'll learn to get your parents off your back, but is that all you want? That's so little. You have bigger dreams, don't you?

> Dream Big!
> This training will make your *whole life easier.*

Dream big, my friend!
You could have freedom, respect, acceptance, and fun.

To paraphrase the first century rabbi, Hillel:

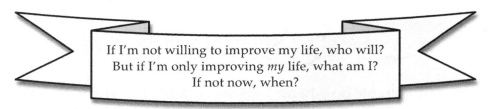

If I'm not willing to improve my life, who will?
But if I'm only improving *my* life, what am I?
If not now, when?

In other words: how long are you willing to wait for your big dreams to start happening? Might as well get the ball rolling now!

H.O.W. IT WORKS

In order to make this whole thing work, you will need three character traits: honesty, open-mindedness, and willingness. (Look! They spell: HOW, like "This is HOW it works!")

This is not about having a good personality. This is about being a person worth spending time with, a person worth respecting.

Your parents love you and you love your parents, but often teens and parents aren't so thrilled with spending time together. *That's because one or both of you aren't honest, open-minded, and willing to listen and learn.*

Sometimes parents and/or teens are dishonest, judgmental, condescending, self-centered, or stubborn. Who wants to hang around that kind of person?

If these adjectives describe your parents, even a little, it's going to take a skilled leader to train them, and that skilled leader can be you!

- ✓ **Honesty** will help you see yourself and your parents as you really are – the great and the not so great. Honesty will help you communicate better with your parents as well.

- ✓ **Open-mindedness** will allow you to find new ways to approach the same old problems. Will you be able to explore new ideas and take new steps?

- ✓ **Willingness** gives you the courage to make changes once you catch a glimpse of what you want to change.

Your brain has a mind of its own

Here's another thing: you will probably want to throw this book across the room at some point. **If you feel rebellious or frustrated with this information, it actually means you're doing *great*.**

> Brains can take in new information but they can also resist because it's too much work.

You know how it can be really nice to go out and have a bunch of fun with your friends, and then it's even nicer to go home and get into comfortable clothes and just watch TV, or take over the video game console, or sleep?

The brain is like that: it can stretch but then it likes to go back to where it was, all relaxed.

When you ask your brain to take in new information, it will stretch to let it all in, but it will also resist. That's why studying or doing homework isn't smooth like going down a fun slide!

Studying is more like going down a rocky slope. At some point, you're going to be in some pain and you're going to say, "Hey! I need a break."

(This is where you might throw the book across the room).

Resistance is natural.
Rebellion is a good thing; it means you're trying hard!

If you need a break, take one, It's fine.
You'll come back to it when you're ready.
Don't push yourself.
This isn't a timed race.
You can go at your own pace and still be successful!

MAKE THIS BOOK YOUR OWN

Feel free to bend the cover, break the binding, write in it, draw pictures, use a pencil or use colored markers.

You can write over or next to the text, or you can use the blank pages in the back.

You might think about buying a journal so you can keep your thoughts private, as I mentioned earlier.

Do what works for you.

Here are some ways you might approach your parent training:

✓ You can read through the whole book first.

✓ You can do each day in a day.

✓ You can do each day in a day and then wait a few days or weeks before continuing

✓ You can take longer than a day for each section.

✓ You can read through the whole book and then put it down for a while and come back to it.
   Or,

✓ You can do a combination of these.

The most important thing is to respect your own rhythm. Trust your gut. Listen to your inner voice. Take a deep breath. Say a prayer. Do whatever works to fortify your soul and then dive in.

So, are you ready for a little boot camp? A course in "What Makes Parents Tick?" "Obedience School for Adults?"

Yes? Then let's get started!

DAY ONE
What's Wrong With Them? Parents Behaving Badly

> "They're too strict. They're embarrassing." Salima, 15
> "I'm almost an adult. I shouldn't have many rules." Dylan, 14

Twelve, thirteen, fourteen years old – it seems you hit a certain age and things veer off into crazy town. Understanding, getting along, and kindness fly out the window. Your parents think you've become an alien and you think they've become prison guards.

Even in homes that are loving and friendly, there's some confusion and a bit of fear about what might be coming.

Parents are asking "What happened and how do we put it back the way it was?"

But things don't change overnight. That's a myth.

Check this out:

If you drop a frog into a pot of boiling water, it'll jump right out. Even if the lid is on, he'll knock it right off.

But if you put a frog into a pot of room temperature water, place the lid on, and turn on the heat, he just sits there, warming up, not realizing that it's getting hotter and hotter.

And in the next instant, that frog is a goner.

11

FAMILIES AT THE BOILING POINT

The frog scenario mirrors the rising temperature (or tension) in families as well.

Room-temperature water: You're going along, having a good time. You're laughing, hugging, and enjoying each other. Occasionally you get into little disagreements. Even less often you get into yelling matches. But these are not serious and you know you love each other.

Bath-water temperature: The yelling happens more frequently. Maybe there's crying involved now. But, hey, you love each other so it will all work out.

Too hot: You start noticing how stupid your parents can be sometimes. Were they always this stupid?

Boiling! Now they're just downright obnoxious. They want to know everything you're doing. They don't trust you anymore. They don't understand you and they're treating you like you're a little kid. Don't they know how old you are?

You're wondering, "What the heck happened?"
And your parents are wondering the same thing.

I don't know where you land regarding the above scenarios, but I can tell you for sure, you and your family are sitting in a pot of water with the heat rising. If you don't do something, you're gonna get burned!

And what a waste. You all deserve better than that, don't you think? *How many years of drama should you have to go through?* I say zero years, but since you're probably in the middle of it, I'm on a search-and-rescue mission to get you outta there!

We'll start easy – some interesting stories, a super tricked-out chart. Just sit back and relax!

TAKING A LOOK AT PARENTS

Let's begin with a good look at your parents: nice-enough folks, except when they're misbehaving.

Some of you will say there are only two types of parents: good parents and bad parents. I'm going to have to disagree with you, only because "good" and "bad" are judgments or opinion statements, and don't really serve our purpose, which is to create a better connection with your parents. Using "good" or "bad," we would say "good" parents don't need fixing, and "bad" parents are beyond help. But there's so much more to this equation.

Likewise, some of you might argue that there are a million types of parents just like there are millions of different people. I'd have to agree with you, but this wouldn't serve our purpose either.

If there are millions of types of parents then how can this book possibly work for you?

The fact is, while parents are of course individuals, what's most important for our purposes is to look at what blocks them from forming a connection with you.

So I've narrowed all those millions of parents into five types; these types identify parenting styles.

Parents put up walls because they're frustrated, confused, and afraid.

Understanding the style of the adults in your life will help you become an "unblocker" for your family (and the one who does the unblocking wins big, my friend!)

SEESAWING BETWEEN JOY AND FEAR

A lot of parenting is a tug-of-war between fear and joy. It's a huge responsibility: your fragile life in their very human and imperfect hands. *Scary*. Plus, parents pretty much carry you around in their hearts and minds 24/7. And when you love someone that much, it's tricky to be impartial or neutral.

When you're out there achieving all over the place, parents feel so good: Joy, Pride, Gratitude, Fun, Whoo Hoo!

But it gets hard when you're being stubborn or whiny, or you're slacking off. That's when parents start freaking out. I know you've seen it.

What you may not realize is that...
Parents Freaking Out = Parents Being Afraid.

- ✓ They may be afraid someone will hurt you.
- ✓ They may be afraid you won't be a happy adult unless you follow their plan for you.
- ✓ They may be afraid of not doing enough to help you become everything you can be.
- ✓ They may not know how to approach you.
- ✓ They may be so busy worrying about you that they forget to look for the good things you're doing.
- ✓ They may be afraid to look like bad parents, and they may think *your* grades are *their* grades! ("My kid got a D! Guess I get a D in parenting then.")
- ✓ They may confuse who *they were* in the past with who *you are* in the present.
- ✓ They may not understand who you are and what you need.
- ✓ They may confuse love with control.
- ✓ They may confuse love with being permissive.

You may have some of this confusion or some of these fears as well, either regarding your parents or someone else you love very much. If so, use those emotions to help you relate to your parents and where they're coming from.

DIFFERENT TYPES OF PARENTS

Even the best parents make mistakes. Even the worst parents do some things right.

Let's look at the different kinds of parents, their core beliefs and values, what they're afraid of, and what that might look like from your point of view.

One thing to note is whatever kind of parents you have, they're probably not like that 100% of the time. Even the best parents make mistakes, and it's pretty typical for a parent to go back and forth between two types.

Also, keep in mind that married couples (or divorced couples) don't always parent the same. Don't be surprised if their types differ!

THE DISCIPLINARIANS

- ✓ Like to have rules for everything
- ✓ Have a punishment for every broken rule
- ✓ Have high and, often, unrealistic expectations
- ✓ Prefer to lecture or direct you rather than discuss things with you
- ✓ Are somewhat formal, or are smothering (*Control has many faces.*)

Parents who are disciplinarians have strong beliefs about how the world (and the family) should operate. Think of a cold, hard ice cube.

> Disciplinarians can control with a frown, a look of concern, or even an overly sweet smile!

Some disciplinarians don't look serious or harsh.

Being over-protective is another way to control a person. It's harder to detect, though, since it's often accompanied by a concerned look or a sweet smile, you know?

The over-protective variety of disciplinarian is often called a *"Helicopter Parent"* because of the way they hover over their kids:

"Honey. Honey. Honey. Honey. It's time to get up. Honey?"

"Oh dear, you look so much better when you brush your hair."

"Go to the bathroom before we leave."

"Take your vitamins."

LOL.

Disciplinarians can have a sweet side too, as long as everyone's doing what they're supposed to be doing. When things get out of hand, however, the yelling and lecturing and the "I'm disappointed in you" starts up.

15

16-year old Kezzy was expected to get good grades, attend church, babysit her younger siblings, and help out her mother around the house.

The only rule she had was, "Do whatever your mother and father tell you to do."

Kezzy's father, Barnard, was so worried that his daughter wouldn't reach her potential that he didn't know what else to do but push her to achieve, achieve, achieve. He would repeatedly tell her that, "People of our race have to do twice as well as everyone else, or we will be ignored."

So for Barnard, obeying meant success. Can you see that it was fear that made him so strict?

And, in a strange way, it was love as well. He just didn't know how to show it.

DISTRACTED PARENTS

- ✓ Get excited by the next new idea or plan (and there's always a new idea or plan)
- ✓ Stress out
- ✓ Like their homes to have some order, but the order can seem random to you
- ✓ Can be critical *or* correcting whenever they pay attention to you
- ✓ Can be affectionate and loving when they're relaxed or on vacation

> Distracted parents have a hard time staying in the moment.

Distracted parents have a hard time parenting because they are often, well, distracted! They are busy, busy, busy, trying to find the solution to whatever is agitating them. That comes first.

Think of a hummingbird, flitting from flower to flower: "Here's some, here's some! Oh, look at this, and this, and this!"

Distracted parents *try* to stay focused on you but they are more comfortable *solving* problems than *listening* to them.

Alan has a hundred good ideas; sometimes, all at once! At work, he may think about everything that would make his family better. At home, he may think about what would make work better. He has a hard time being present, just sitting and enjoying what is.

Alan is happier thinking about what *could* be.

His family is often agitated because they're not sure what his mood will be from hour to hour, let alone from day to day. *But Alan does love his kids and his wife. He just doesn't like to be interrupted from his "important" tasks.*

He forgets that he needs to slow down and turn his brain off. He doesn't see that it's his moodiness and unreliability that create frustration and sadness in his loved ones.

PERMISSIVE PARENTS

- ✓ Don't like to enforce rules (or even have rules, sometimes)
- ✓ Really want to be a friend rather than a parent
- ✓ Believe kids learn better from experiencing life, come what may
- ✓ Think childhood is pretty much all about having as much fun as possible
- ✓ Value independent thought and action above everything else

The permissive parent is often considered "the F-U-N parent" or "the friend." Sometimes teens think this is the best type of parent because there are few rules and expectations.

You know how confetti is so colorful and fun? That's the cool part of having a permissive parent. Unfortunately, just like with confetti, permissive parents can create messes (parenting messes) that are a pain to clean up.

> Whoa. Margit's bringing it!

Yes I am.

Permissive parents often secretly (or not so secretly) resent being the adult. Responsibility scares them so much that they pretend that being a friend is the same as being a good parent. They fear not being liked by their children.

17

Carol's motto is, "Let kids have fun. This is the only time they'll have to be kids." And she enjoys being one of the kids too. She uses raunchy slang, she burps, and she shakes her booty. Carol's home has few rules.

But without any rules, her kids are failing school and, in turn, Carol feels they have betrayed and disrespected her.

So what does she do? **She works harder to be her kids' friend!**
Now she is parenting from a place of fear, resentment and shame.
Not a good combination.

EVEN-HANDED PARENTS

✓ Love their children and let them know it
✓ Balance responsibility and fun
✓ Respond to misbehavior in a firm yet kind manner
✓ Know that yelling, lecturing, and nagging are pointless
✓ Are emotionally healthy and value the emotional growth of their children

Okay, I'm going to be honest: the even-handed parent is my favorite kind of parent, the kind I'd wish for every child.

Being even-handed, they are flexible yet dependable. There aren't loads of conflicts with even-handed parents, not because it's easy to stand up to them and win an argument, but because *they don't want to argue.*
They just want to parent!

> Even-handed parents are quieter. Just sayin'…

Diana is a wonderful mother. One of my favorites. Sure, she has rules, but her family also has loads of fun.

When the rules are broken, Diana is pretty calm. She'll simply ask, "Can you tell me what happened?" And then when her daughter Amanda finishes explaining, Diana will say, "We have a rule about that, so what's next?"

And Amanda tells her mom what her own consequence is!

(More about Diana in a bit)

DISCONNECTED PARENTS

They can be any or all of these:
- ✓ Super angry
- ✓ Physically or verbally abusive
- ✓ Severely depressed
- ✓ Drinking a lot or abusing medications or illegal drugs
- ✓ Mentally ill in another way

A disconnected parent is like a sleeping bear. Never poke a sleeping bear. They do not want their world disturbed.

Most disconnected parents love their children deeply but they are adults stuck in their own worlds. They are usually not bad people, but they are in emotional pain and need professional help.

Kids of disconnected parents carry lots of pain. It's hard to live with instability.

If you have a disconnected parent, you know something is wrong, but they may try to convince you that *you're* the problem. And, often, you believe it.

Disconnected parents are very hard to live with, partly because sometimes they *can* connect. Sometimes they can be nice, and sometimes they can be attentive to their children's needs.

At those times, it's hard for a son or daughter not to get their hopes up. But then, without help, a disconnected parent hits another bottom, disconnects, and leaves the child hanging without a "safety net."

It's a real roller coaster.

Let's revisit Diana who, it turns out, is **part even-handed and part disconnected parent,** but she handles her moods in a *healthy* way.

Diana herself will tell you that sometimes she needs to disconnect. When life feels too big, she tells her family, "I need to go take a break/nap/walk. I'll rejoin you in an hour or so."

Notice that it's not the family's fault. With most disconnected parents it's not the family's fault. Diana has learned not to hurt or confuse the people she loves. In fact, she is being reliable and trustworthy.

19

It's ironic that many teens think their parents are disconnected, when actually they're not at all. There's just a huge communication gap, a gap this book can mend.

If you know people who have disconnected parents, it's crucial that they find a trustworthy adult to talk to. There's a short piece at the end of this book: *Is Anybody Listening? Five Tips for Finding Trustworthy Adults.* It's a good read for any young adult. Check it out.

Here's a chart comparing the five types of parents.

Remember, parents can often act like a couple different types, as we have seen above, but one type usually stands out more than the others.

Parenting Types → / Characteristics ↓	Disciplinarian	Distracted	Permissive	Even-Handed	Disconnected
Core value	Doing things the right way	A busy life is a good life	Freedom	Emotional health	Control
Core belief	Following societal or family standards is the key to success	When I feel better, the family will feel better.	Parents who make rules are heartless	Parent with kindness *and* firmness	Life is hard. I do what I have to in order to handle it
Fears	If my kids don't do what they're supposed to do, they will be failures	I don't want my kids to have problems, so I'll get some answers now	I don't want to be like my parents. I'm afraid my kids won't like me	I don't want my kids to grow up unprepared for life's joys and challenges	If I don't get what I need and want, I'll flip out
Behavior	Can be over-protective and/or strict and cold	Worried, spacey, forgetful or irritable	Seems much more like one of the kids than like a parent	Loving, fun, dependable and responsible	Random. May be threatening and/or neglectful

PARENTING SYNERGY

Now you've got a ton of information.
Big deal. What now?

Well, you've already read that I'm a big fan of the even-handed parent, and that I think the permissive parent isn't really doing a good job at all. But why?

Let me show you!

I came up with this sort of theory called Parenting Synergy. Synergy (pronounced: SIN-er-jee) means how things work (or play) together best.

The synergy between two things creates something greater than the two things by themselves.

> Synergy is the connection or cooperation between two different people or things.

You know how you can have a really good friend and you just feel like you're a better person when you're around him or her?

That's synergy; two people "work" together and create something more awesome than if they were alone.

Synergy needs a connection of two different things.

MAGNETS ATTRACT OR REPEL

Now think about two magnets: when you place the two negative poles end-to-end, they repel one another. The same thing happens when you place the two positive poles together.

They can only attract one another if the positive end is put together with the negative end.

You know there's nothing you can do to force a connection between the same two ends. It just won't work. (You can try this with two magnets if you want.)

Now imagine that one end of the magnet represents the parent and the other end, the child. If both the parent-ends of the magnet try to connect, they can't. If both the child-ends of the magnet try to connect, they can't either.

HOW DOES SYNERGY WORK IN PARENTING?

What happens in many parent-child relationships is that there *can't be synergy* because either the parent expects the child to be an adult ("Why can't you be more responsible?"), or the parent wants to be a child along with his or her own children ("You can figure out your own rules. You're probably just as smart as I am.")

(Hey, can you read that paragraph again? Aloud would be even better. It's a super important paragraph).

But, but, but... in parenting, for there to be Synergy, one of you has to be the parent and one of you has to be the child, and it's usually better if the parent is the adult and the child is, well, you!

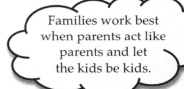

Families work best when parents act like parents and let the kids be kids.

When this happens, the connection that can be created is beyond belief – better than you or your parents can imagine!

Take another look at our chart on page 20.

You can see that **disciplinarian parents** pretty much want their kids to be adults. There isn't much room for fun or hanging out. This is why teens with disciplinarian parents may rebel – kids want to be kids! I know you've also seen kids crack under the pressure of having to be mini-adults.

You can also see that **permissive parents** don't want to be authority figures – they would rather join their children and connect as two children (or two teens).

But according to Parenting Synergy, someone has to be the parent. It's sad when the child ends up being the adult. The kids may have to remind their parents of the daily schedule or chores that need to be done.

It's too darn hard to figure out the rules of the adult world when you're a kid. It's even hard when you're a teen. *(Frankly, it's sometimes hard to figure out the adult world even when you're an adult!)* We need adults to be adults so that you can learn how to be future adults. Or else, who's going to teach you?

The only family where the adult is the parent and the teen gets to be a teen – the only family where there's Synergy – is where there's an **Even-handed parent.** (Yeah, read that one again too - might as well.) Even-handed parents are able to get their emotional needs met by other adults; they don't need their children to make them "look good," so they're perfectly happy being the adults while their children just get to be themselves.

What about the **distracted and disconnected parent?** Both of them are often so focused on themselves that they detach from the family much of the time, *refusing to be either parent or child.* They have their own lives to think about, but will occasionally "come up for air" and randomly be critical or loving.

Often, children with one of these parents will look to another parent, stepparent, or responsible adult for support, guidance, and love. Fortunately, kids and teens can thrive when there's at least one loving and trustworthy adult around to rely on.

THINKING ABOUT YOUR OWN FAMILY

How do you see the adults in your life? Do you have an aunt or uncle who is very permissive? Do you have a grandparent who is disconnected? How about a parent or stepparent who is even-handed?

Which types do you recognize in your own family?

Take some time to think about this. You might want to circle or highlight some descriptions in the chart on page 20, or take some notes in a journal, or use the blank pages at the end of this book.

Try writing about a specific time when each of these adults did something (good or bad) that that type of parent would do. How did you feel when those things happened?

I'm not asking so I can find out your darkest secrets. I just want *you* to see where your parents (or other adults) may need some BOOT CAMP!

For instance, did any fear or anger come up when you looked at the chart? It's okay to feel either one. Parenting is certainly challenging, but so is being a young person with a parent, so it's natural to feel some resentment or disappointment, for instance, if you discover things could be going a lot better than they are.

That's what this book is for – to help you become an expert on your parents so you can turn them into something much more enjoyable and much less stressful.

Take some time to write out your feelings. Remember what Einstein said. Even though you're intelligent, you can't solve a problem if it stays in your head.

THINKING ABOUT DAY ONE:

In Day One you learned that assumptions, insecurities, fear of losing control, and miscommunication are the causes of family tension. You also looked at different types of parents and learned the theory of Parenting Synergy.

What was the most helpful thing you learned in Day One?

What's one thing you learned that you think your best friend would find most interesting? How about your siblings? Your parents?

As you continue through this book, you'll be collecting new ways to think and act. You'll be more confident and more comfortable with who you are and where you're going in the world.

And, amazingly, so will your parents!

P.S. If you're feeling a bit overwhelmed or confused, I suggest you read (or re-read) the introduction.

You don't have to do all this in one day if you don't want to. You can take your time.

Keeping the days in order, however, is very important.

On to Day Two – Keep rockin' and rollin'!

DAY TWO
Parental Paranoia: It's What's For Breakfast!

"My dad is chill but my mom is always yelling." Tran, 13

"My father has a lot of money and thinks he can run
his family like he runs his company." Marcus, 18

Have you ever stopped to think about how hard it is to parent?

I mean, sure, there are huge benefits. Like you get to watch someone grow and develop skills, and become this magical, miraculous being who makes friends, goes to school, conquers challenges, and looks so beautiful when asleep.

Poet Elizabeth Stone wrote:

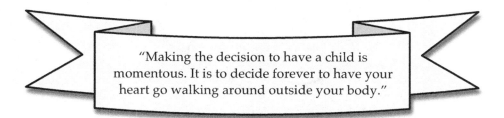

"Making the decision to have a child is momentous. It is to decide forever to have your heart go walking around outside your body."

Think about that. I mean, *helloooo!* It's dangerous to have your heart go walking around outside your body. It could get hurt!

Have you ever loved anybody so much? Maybe it's a parent or other relative. Maybe it's a pet or a close friend. Take a moment, close your eyes, and really feel the love. Some of you may have to go back a few years, but I know the love is there.

Now, what if you had to send those beloved beings out into the world on their own?

You can't go with them.
You have to trust that the world will be kind to them, and…
You have to *suspend disbelief and pretend to believe* that if there's any danger, they'll be able to spot it and avoid it.

Can you imagine how that might make parents feel very vulnerable and very fearful? After all, in the ironic words of author William Burroughs:

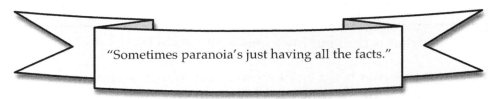

"Sometimes paranoia's just having all the facts."

Maybe parents have a right to be afraid? Maybe Parental Paranoia is a level of *excellence* for which we should be grateful?!

"AM I A GOOD-ENOUGH PARENT?"

Parents spend a lot of time thinking about you, and questioning whether they are doing a good-enough job, and feeling guilty that they can't do better.

Your parents are wondering if they're "good enough" ALL THE TIME.

"Did we teach him the right things?"
"Is he safe?"
"Will someone be mean to her?"
"Are we strict enough?"
"Are we too strict?"
"What if we die?"
"What if she gets sick or injured?"

There's so much to worry about when you've loved someone for so long. And remember, your parents haven't just loved you the length of your life. Many parents dreamed of having kids long, long before you were born. *They loved you before you were even conceived.* That's a looooooooooong time, wouldn't you say?

Still, you would think that, having been teens themselves, they would understand you more, and they'd get it right more often.

Don't they remember how many things there are to think about every day?

✓ Do I look okay?
✓ Do I smell okay?
✓ Am I normal?
✓ Is there anything I forgot at home?
✓ Will this person, that person, or the other person be at school today?
✓ Is anyone talking about me?
✓ If so, what are they saying?
✓ If not, what's wrong with me?
✓ Besides all that, what's wrong with me?

Do parents have any idea how complicated your life is?

The answer is "yes" and "no." Not a very satisfactory answer, but it's the truth. Just like you, parents have hundreds of decisions to make every day. And, just like you, they're thinking about stuff like, "Do I look okay?" "Are people talking about me?"
And, of course, your parents were teens once too, so it's not like they're raising an alien.

But here's the weird part: you kind of go through life thinking about your life and your needs and what you want to do. Well, guess what? Your parents do too!

Here's a list of what parents think about:

✓ *Your* life

✓ *Your* needs

✓ What you want to do now

✓ What you want to do in the future

✓ How to make enough money to give you the life you deserve

✓ How to be strong for you

✓ How to be healthy for you (and also for themselves)

✓ How to find solutions so they don't have to bug you with their problems

✓ Should they praise you or will that embarrass you?

✓ If they don't praise you, will you think they don't care or don't love you?

✓ If they get angry, will it help?

✓ If they don't get angry, will it help?

✓ Is it okay if you fail?

✓ If not, what should they do to prevent you from failing?

✓ Is this a phase, or are you always going to be this unhappy/angry/underachieving/spacey/bored/dishonest/mean?

✓ If they make a wrong decision *here or here or here or here,* how will it affect your future, and will you all still have a relationship when you're older? And . . .

✓ *All of the above, all over again, for each and every kid and step kid in your family.*

Pretty crazy list, isn't it?

Did you have any idea how much your parents think about you and your well-being?

It's a wonder that parents' brains don't explode. They have to think about themselves, each other, their friends, their work, the state of the world, and you and your siblings.

When do they relax? And *how* do they relax? Parenting is a big ball of stress, don't you think?

You can see why they need training, can't you? ☺

ADOLESCENCE, THE SEQUEL

Back to Parental Paranoia. Here's another big concern parents have: the whole time you're busy being a teen, your parents are remembering their *own* childhood.

They're raising you and watching you triumph and fail and, at the same time, they're thinking about how they were raised and how they triumphed and, *especially*, how they *failed.*

Unconsciously, they may be envious that you get opportunities they didn't have, or that you are good at something they were bad at.

> *To summarize:*
> Parents get stressed
> but it's okay.
> You'll understand
> when you're a parent.

They're also thinking about their bad behavior and want to make very sure you don't get away with what they got away with, or that you don't make the same mistakes. (It's true. I hear it all the time.)

It's complex and parents may not want to talk about it with you, but the outside world is a shocking place when you're a parent. You may just need to accept that, know it's not all about you, and move on.

NEGATIVE THINKING HURTS YOU

But . . .

Even though they're demanding and paranoid and screechy and unreasonable, it doesn't help you at all to think of them as stupid, crazy, broken-down robots.

In fact, even though it seems pretty innocent and harmless, this kind of negative thinking actually hurts you. (This is so important that I'm saying it several times!)

Your thoughts are your most powerful friends and weapons. They influence your present and future, oftentimes even more than your brain chemistry, your upbringing, your physical limitations, and your environment.

> ← Read

Here, I'm writing this paragraph again. It took me 'til the age of 35 to learn this. I don't want you to have to wait that long:

> Read it again
> →

Your thoughts are your most powerful friends and weapons. They influence your present and future, oftentimes even more than your brain chemistry, your upbringing, your physical limitations, and your environment.

(Seriously, you should copy it and post it everywhere so you don't forget).

Just think about all the success stories you've ever read or heard about: people with learning and physical disabilities, people from horribly dysfunctional families, people raised in extreme poverty.

In **100%** of those stories, you also hear about how they had a positive attitude, they refused to give up, and when things got tough they asked for help.

You never hear anyone say, "Yeah, so I had a crappy attitude and just sat around, but hundreds of people magically appeared to help me, and it all turned out great!"

*They had to at least **pretend** to have a good attitude even if they didn't fully buy it.*
And you do too.

PICK A THEME, ANY THEME

So here's an easy exercise you can do for the rest of your life. E-A-S-Y. And power-packed.

And it will improve your attitude (even if it's already pretty good) by helping you focus on the positive.

You can also teach it to anyone of almost any age.

All you do is pick a theme for the day or week or month or year, and set up reminders so you don't forget.

Themes? What's that mean?

Okay, so in this fun exercise, a theme can be a **personality trait** like: friendly, tolerant, forgiving, calm, trustworthy (and many more)

OR

it can be an **action** you want to do more, like: studying, exercising, eating healthy, not swearing, playing more with my younger siblings, and so on

OR

it can describe a **role** you play (or want to play) in the world, like: artist, scientist, healer, friend, learner, etc.

OR

it can be a **quality** you want to embody: harmony, freedom, non-judgment, love, prosperity – the possibilities are endless

OR

you can take a **line or phrase** from a book, movie, or song.

Needless to say, they should be positive themes, *not* like "judgmental," "class clown," "irritating stepson," "couch-potato," or "I like violence" (I made up that last one. I have no idea if it's in a book, movie, or song lyric).

Next, you make a deck of cards. It doesn't matter how many cards are in the deck. That's totally up to you. You can use 3 x 5 cards or just pieces of paper. You can use a deck of cards covered in plain paper. On each card, you write one theme. Whichever you like.

Here are some of my personal favorites:

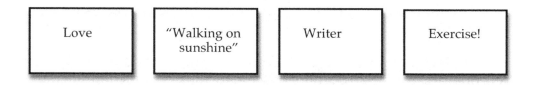

So, let's say on Monday, I pick the "Love" card. That means that, to the best of my ability, that day I'm going to focus on Love, no matter what else happens. If a friend or family member is having a hard time and taking it out on me, I will reciprocate with Love. Period. Love, love, love, love, love!

Or, let's say on Tuesday I choose "Writer." That means I need to make sure to make time for writing that day, even if it's only for an hour or two. Writer, writer, writer, writer.

Then, every day (or week, or month, or year) you pick a new theme. You can use any or all types of themes described above. I think it's more fun when you have at least 25 themes to choose from and you do it every day.

Here are a few ways to remind yourself:

- ✓ Make a screen-saver reminder
- ✓ Make a computer-wallpaper reminder
- ✓ Have your phone remind you periodically
- ✓ Make a calendar reminder with a message
- ✓ Put it on a white board
- ✓ Put up a sign
- ✓ Carry the card with you
- ✓ Make it your Facebook status (that's one of the things we're doing on the @TrainUrParents FB page)

With your thoughts consistently directed toward a theme, you become more confident, less stressed, and more likeable. Yup, all that.

MIRROR NEURONS. AWESOMENESS.

More about having a good attitude and such: you know when you have a teacher who's pretty negative, you feel down or resentful or bored, right? Likewise, when you have a teacher who is enthusiastic, they can make a boring subject bearable and, even, fun.

This happens all the time in families too – negative thinking creates more negative thinking, and positive thinking creates more positive thinking.

In fact (and this is so cool) there are things called "Mirror Neurons" in your brain that unconsciously make people imitate the people they're around. The presence of mirror neurons explains why, when someone yawns, many of us also yawn. We're *mirroring* them. >> (Some of you are yawning right now. I did that to you! Heh.) <<

And this is why it's so important to change your thinking when you're training your parents.

If you try to train them while thinking, "They're too dumb to get it," their mirror neurons will activate and mimic your negative thoughts, *even if those thoughts are silent.* I'm not kidding.

If you approach their training with a positive thought like, "This is going to be fun. I can't wait to see what happens!" their mirror neurons will tell them, "Hey, something fun is coming up!"

This also applies to thoughts you have about yourself, so BE NICE!

It's cool, right?
You've got so much more power than you thought.

Negative thoughts about a person put up a wall that makes it pretty much *impossible to connect* with them.

It's like saying, "You're not worth my time!" So they either avoid you or they keep trying to change you.

WHAT NEGATIVE THOUGHTS ABOUT YOUR PARENTS ARE YOU HOLDING ONTO??

What negative thoughts and judgments are you carrying around about your parents?
What would you like to change about them?

I know those judgments are in there.
It's okay.
It's normal.
You're not a bad person.

At the same time, I know that anger and resentment do more damage to the person feeling them (you) than to the person they're directed at (a parent, or whomever). *Sometimes the other person doesn't even know you're mad at them.* They just keep on living the good life, and your blood pressure is rising!

The spiritual teacher, Buddha, wrote:

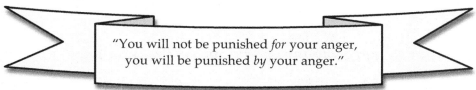

"You will not be punished *for* your anger, you will be punished *by* your anger."

So let's release some steam, so to speak, bring that B.P. down, and talk about the stuff we think is very bad to talk about:

What bugs you about your parents?

35

Below are some complaints I hear regularly from teens.

Feel free to add your own. Get as many out as you can think of. If you hold on to any, your parent training won't work as well.

Wanna write? Sure! Brilliant idea. Do some writing about what bugs you. It doesn't mean you're right, but writing won't hurt them, and it'll help you. You're just writing, not sharing.

- ✓ They spend more time criticizing me than being nice to me.
- ✓ They're too tired to do fun stuff.
- ✓ They yell too much.
- ✓ Our house is a mess and I'm embarrassed to bring friends over.
- ✓ They forget stuff and then blame me for it.
- ✓ My sister/brother has it way easier than I do.
- ✓ They're embarrassing.

- ✓ _____
- ✓ _____
- ✓ _____
- ✓ _____
- ✓ _____

Now comes the good part. (I wouldn't leave you hanging with all those complaints on your mind, that's for sure!)

THOUGHT FLIPPING (PREPARE TO BE AMAZED . . .)

I ♥ "Thought Flipping." It requires zero skills and works even if you don't believe it'll work. That is my kind of activity!

Plus, it's super easy and it works in lots of different situations. This is a skill you're going to want to remember for sure.

For example, after college-student Maya had a car accident, she was a bit nervous about driving. I taught her that instead of thinking,

"I'm going to be killed! I just know it!" she should repeat over and over, "I am safe. My car is safe. I am safe. My car is safe." She hasn't had an accident since. True story (but the names have been changed throughout this book. To protect the innocent, of course.)

I showed teen-client Max how to do this with his grades ("I'm smart. I can pass any test I study for.") And he started getting As and Bs instead of Ds and Fs. Also a true story.

Crazy? Not really. But it is a bit odd, I know.

Parents have trouble believing me as well.
Wouldn't it be nice if they had the courage to try some thought-flipping themselves? Instead of thinking, "My child is bugging me!" they would flip that thought to "My child and I get along great!"

But this isn't their book; it's yours, and I believe you have plenty of courage to handle this exercise.
All you have to do is just flip your thinking!

So, try it. You can change the negative thought, "My parents criticize me a lot" to "My parents compliment me a lot."

This is another exercise that seems too simple. It doesn't make sense.

"My parents try to understand me, and I take time to try to understand my parents."

But it works. You start focusing on the good stuff your parents do, and lo and behold, they actually start doing more good stuff and saying more positive things to you.

Your turn!

Try some of your own Thought Flipping. Start with the negative thought and flip it:

>*Thought:* My parents think I'm stupid.

Flip: My parents know I'm smart.

>*Thought:* I hate being around my parents.

Flip: I like being around my parents.

Thought: _____

Flip: _____

Thought: _____

Flip: _____

Try repeating each of the positive phrases five times each, three times a day, for the rest of the day, and into the upcoming weeks and months. Don't stop, or the magic will just fade away. ☺

If that much work scares you, do less. Take your time.
But know that the more you practice, the better things will become - and sooner.

THINKING ABOUT DAY TWO:

In Day Two you learned why parents can be so paranoid: they love you tons, they want to be the best parents ever, and they aren't sure how to do that. You learned they can't help themselves and that you really shouldn't fight it or you'll be fighting forever!

Also we talked about the (daily, weekly, etc) Theme exercise and Mirror Neurons (more on that in the Credits section at the end of the book) and you practiced Thought-Flipping. Powerful, yet simple, exercises. Plus, I hope you practiced a bit, if not today then certainly before you get started on Day Three.

Training your parents is going to require you to venture outside of your comfort zone, and for many of us, these exercises are a first step.

What good changes have you noticed from the Theme exercise or from flipping your thoughts?

What was the most helpful thing you learned in Day Two?

What's one thing you learned that you think your best friend would find most interesting? How about your siblings? Your parents?

If you're feeling a bit overwhelmed, try some Thought-Flipping around those feelings. For instance, instead of saying, "There's no way this stuff is going to work!" or "It's too hard!" try flipping your thoughts and declare: "This *is* going to work!" and "I can do this!"

'Coz it will.
And you can.

DAY THREE
Can You See Me Now? Teens, Parents, and Stereotypes

> "They never listen, they won't let boys stay over,
> and they don't trust me!" Kenya, 15
>
> "They ask too many questions! They're always
> in my business like they don't trust me." Truong, 15

On Day One we looked at what types of parents there are. To start Day Three, let's look at the types *(or stereotypes)* of teens there are, *from a parent's point of view.* Why are we looking at you as a stereotype? We want you to understand what parents see *when they think of teens.*

Types of teens → Characteristics ↓	"Lazy"	"Goofball"	"Gangster"	"Goody Two Shoes"	"Normal"
Core Value	Nothing	Having fun	Chaos	Getting approval	Self-fulfillment
Likes	Sleeping, eating, TV, computer games	Sleeping, eating, friends	Vandalism, drugs, hurting people	Kissing up to teachers, obeying parents	Good grades, friends, family
Dislikes	Doing anything productive	School, paying attention	Not having power	People who waste time	Mean people
Parents' Advice	*DO something with your life!*	*FOCUS!*	They're too scared of their kids to give advice	*Don't you want to have any fun?*	*Keep up the good work!*

It may not be fair.

It may not be correct.

But it will be helpful to understand this, and then train that stuff out of your parents' brains! (And just to show you how confused parents are – they also don't want a Goody Two-Shoes, no-personality kid either!)

Have you ever heard an adult ask someone: "Why do you have to be so lazy/disrespectful/stupid/mean/irritating/moody/distant (any of those)? Why can't you be more *this* or *that* or *the other thing*, like a *NORMAL* person?"

Calling something "normal" doesn't really mean anything. What's normal? (My friend, Kay, says 'Normal' is just a setting on the washing machine. LOL)

I mean, for some parents, a "normal" teen argues and sulks and is a pain to live with. For other parents, "normal" means obedient and easy-to-parent.

Aren't these both stereotypes?

Still, if parents had their way, you'd all be . . .

hardworking, brilliant, popular, happy, kind, well groomed, funny, resourceful, creative, adaptable, reasonable, and fun.

Not much to ask for, is it?

The thing parents don't remember is that people aren't *born* motivated and hardworking and reasonable, and most of those other things. It's UNreasonable of them to expect this from you!

Of course, this is another reason why you need to train them: Parents *also* need to remember to be reasonable and adaptable and kind!

TYPES OF TEENS

So let's put together a better "Types of Teens" chart, and then we'll talk more about the different types that show up.

As with the Types of Parents chart on page 20, this chart focuses on the different ways teens connect (or don't connect) with their parents.

Types of Teens → / Characteristics ↓	Disconnected	Compliant	Rebellious	"Passive–Aggressive"	Cooperative
Core value	Simplicity	Peace and quiet	Respect	To be seen and heard	Getting along with people
Something the teen might say	"I just want to feel normal"	"I'm not looking for trouble"	"I won't respect them if they don't respect me first"	"They don't understand"	"I finished my chores and homework"
Teen's fear is:	Never feeling okay again	Being noticed—it may mean rejection or ridicule	They're not worth respecting	Not being understood or valued	Not feeling close to their parents
How teen gets attention from parents	Being super needy or super quiet	By doing whatever is asked	Arguing and defiance	*Bending* the rules	Just by being themselves

Parents try to connect by telling you stuff. They're kinda big on talking, whether it's lecturing, yelling, or swearing at you.

For teens, the tendency is to connect by trying to get attention. And why not?

Positive attention is G-R-R-R-E-A-T, but teens often end up getting negative attention – scolding and criticism – and then can't stop their behavior because bad attention (sigh) is better than no attention at all.

Or is it?

Did you know you can get good attention and still be your rockin' self?

Most kids tend to connect by trying to get attention. But are you going for *good* attention?

Stick with me; this is one of my areas of expertise!

DISCONNECTED TEENS

They can be:
- ✓ Developmentally challenged
- ✓ Severely depressed or anxious
- ✓ Living in poverty
- ✓ Participating in illegal activities, including violence
- ✓ Very caught up in drugs, alcohol, sex, cutting, tech/gaming, binge eating or other disordered eating behaviors such as food restricting, vomiting, or over-exercising.

Unlike with disconnected parents, disconnected teens often can't help themselves, other than telling someone they need help and then hoping the person won't laugh at them (scary).

Think of a landline telephone whose cord has been cut. The phone could work just fine if the cord was intact. That's what I mean by "disconnected."

Some disconnected teens know they're disconnected. If you are struggling with depression or anxiety, if you're poor, or if you're trapped in addictive behavior, you feel like you're standing outside the world looking in and watching everyone else have fun.

Disconnected teens aren't necessarily trying to get attention. Some are scared of their parents. Most are just trying to get through the day.

Ella got a scholarship to a prestigious university. She loved living in her new city but the pressure of being a freshman with a scholarship was too much for her. She began bingeing and purging – Bulimia – ordering a pint of ice cream, vomiting it up, and then eating cookies. And that was just for breakfast.

After a short time, studying was out of the question. She couldn't concentrate. She also couldn't maintain her friendships because she was filled with such shame.

She was disconnected.

COMPLIANT TEENS

Many teens confuse "compliance" with "cooperation." Compliant teens aren't cooperative. Rather they are meek and submissive.

They are hoping to get "good attention" as the "good son" or "good daughter," but they'd be happy escaping attention altogether, particularly if their parent is a disciplinarian or is disconnected.

Compliant teens have little connection with their parents. They don't think for themselves; they just do what they're told because it's easier and safer than to do otherwise. Compliant teens may also be afraid of their parents.

Compliant Teens are often:
- ✓ Quiet
- ✓ Guarded (he or she doesn't show or share feelings)
- ✓ Shy
- ✓ Not confident
- ✓ Kind to others

Finn is a compliant teen. His parents both drink and this makes him extremely uncomfortable. His father, in particular, gets very angry when he's drunk, and Finn wants to avoid being the target of that anger.

Finn does what he's told and doesn't make waves. He loves his parents deeply but you wouldn't say they have a great relationship.

My fear for Finn is that he won't learn how to connect closely with anyone. You can't be a good friend or spouse if you're used to hiding a lot.

Also, how will he connect with his own kids since his own role model (his father) is someone who's disconnected?

REBELLIOUS TEENS

Teens may be rebellious for quite a few reasons: there may be trouble at home such as alcoholism, a divorce, abuse, a financial upheaval or, as very often happens, the parent is too permissive (ignoring parenting duties) and the teen rebels.

My take is that the rebellious teen is trying to get the parent to step up and *be the parent* – a fair-minded, loving, yet firm family leader.

I see this in my school work as well. Ideally, classrooms are safe places to learn, but when the teacher doesn't have good boundaries and standards, students are more likely to take advantage of the situation and act out to get the teacher to step up and *be* what a teacher is supposed to be – interesting, cheery, firm and caring.

> Where there's a rebel, there's a parent who's not doing his/her best. That's the reason for the rebellion!

I'm sure you've seen how "Aidan" or "Ashley" terrorize one teacher but are cooperative in another class. Of course this means that rebellious kids (who are not also disconnected) have some control over their behavior!

Rebellious teens can be:
- ✓ Sarcastic
- ✓ Disruptive
- ✓ Defiant
- ✓ Impolite
- ✓ Mean

Isaac.

His mother was the permissive one; his dad was the disciplinarian.

Isaac *wanted to be cooperative* but every time he tried, his mother would praise him and then his father would make fun of him and call him a "Mama's Boy," or tease him about something else. (Really.)

So Isaac would just be a jerk back. Like, "I can be a bigger jerk than you, Dad!"

Once I got the father to stop teasing him, Isaac calmed down and became his awesome self.

Rebellious teens, in the extreme, are the bullies of the world. They may bully kids with teasing, fighting, or cruel language.

They will also bully adults by misbehaving in an exaggerated way: screaming at them, mocking what their parents say, or calling them names, for example.

I have found that this situation is so dysfunctional that these families need intensive therapy, sometimes for each member separately. (Neither parents nor kids should be afraid of the other.)

And there is *almost always* some addiction and/or history of abuse in the parents or the grandparents. KIDS NEED TO FEEL SAFE (or they'll let you know, that's for sure)!

PASSIVE-AGGRESSIVE TEENS

The passive-aggressive teen is the most complicated, partly because they are both Passive and Aggressive, and those two traits don't seem to go together. It's like saying someone is both nice and mean. How can that be? *These teens create a bit of unrest at home or at school but not in a forceful or obviously mean way.*

In fact, passive-aggressive teens may have sweet dispositions until they feel pushed, nagged, or merely ignored. Then they react!

If you look back at the Types of Teens chart on page 43, you can see this type of teen just wants to be heard and understood.

Can you hear me now? Can you hear me now? Can you hear me **NOW?**

A passive-aggressive teen will try to get attention by bending the rules as much as possible to get adults to notice them. Sometimes they break rules but, often, that's accidental.

Passive-aggressive teens may be sneaky but they don't want to be seen as rebellious.

While the rebellious teen feels controlled and betrayed by authority, the passive-aggressive teen thinks adults are gullible and can be fooled, or they think themselves equal to adults in intelligence. *In fact, they may see their disruptions as intellectual exercises.*

Passive-aggressive teens may:

✓ Steal
- o Stealing small items – sort of "power tokens" – such as a small amount of money that can possibly go undetected
- o Borrowing things without asking, or using items or equipment when they're not supposed to (Xbox, anyone?)
- o Stealing attention or time to distract or confuse the adult

✓ Lie

✓ Cheat (a form of lying)

✓ Disrupt
- o Interrupting conversations
- o Playing the victim, taking attention (and sympathy) away from an adult or another child
- o Ignoring homework assignments, thus upsetting parents

✓ Distract
- o Making distracting noises, even singing
- o Starting a conversation before anyone else can, so as to control the room
- o Telling jokes to control the mood
- o Twisting or reinterpreting the directions or suggestions given by adults so they benefit the teen

The passive-aggressive teen often confuses parents. They can't figure out if they are too strict or too lenient. This is partly because passive-aggressive teens are good at playing with people's heads. They can act calmly and sound reasonable without being reasonable at all. Then parents start to question their own thinking.

If you are a passive-aggressive teen (as I was!), you know exactly what I'm talking about and you're probably very proud of your intellect. Am I right?

> Mari hoards candy in her bedroom.
> Kenya lies about having a boyfriend.
> Ethan hums whenever his parents try to talk to him seriously.
> Jack is the class clown – he really wants his teachers to like him.
> Gabe tries to negotiate EVERYTHING!

It's not all about the teen though. Like the rebellious teen, the passive-aggressive teen is often the son or daughter of a distracted or frazzled parent who is having his or her own issues. Kids need and deserve lots of attention, but this is confusing, frustrating and exhausting for some parents.

What's important to know is that passive-aggressive teens are insecure about whether they are heard and valued, but they are *not trying to hurt anyone*. They just want to feel good about themselves. They want to belong.

COOPERATIVE TEENS

The definition of cooperative is "working or acting together willingly for a common purpose or benefit."

Cooperative teens don't think their parents are right all the time but they respect their parents and know their parents respect them.

Sounds kinda great, doesn't it?

> Live the dream!
> Be cooperative.

You get to be yourself and people like it. That's pretty much *my* dream!

Cooperative teens tend to:
- ✓ Be happier
- ✓ Have more self-confidence
- ✓ Be more loving
- ✓ Get more respect and trust from their parents
- ✓ Enjoy more independence (Yup. That's what I said.)

As I mentioned before, cooperative teens are not the same as compliant teens – the submissive ones who would rather stay quiet than speak and be rejected or ridiculed.

Cooperative teens aren't submissive at all. They may be quiet, calm, and easy-going, or they may be enthusiastic, boisterous, and energetic. But they're not doing it to get attention. They already have attention; they already feel like they belong.

Cooperative teens that are having a bad day (or week or month!) often self-sabotage (mess things up for themselves) just because they're tired, anxious, feeling insecure, or they're disappointed with something.

Tali and Daya are smart, spirited, and usually cooperative.

Tali has ADHD but she loads her schedule with ridiculously hard classes and time-consuming activities that wear her out and challenge her self-esteem.

When Tali is having a hard time, she self-sabotages by staying up too late and waiting 'til the last minute to get her work done. Cooperative Tali turns into passive-aggressive Tali.

Daya also takes challenging courses but she doesn't have ADHD and her after-school schedule isn't as packed as Tali's.

When Daya feels pressured by tests and homework, she goes into passive-aggressive mode too. Daya will start telling lies and become disruptive at home.

Teens can go through more than one type in a day or week, much more often than parents go through *their* types. Anxiety is a common reason for teens to change types. It's an unconscious coping mechanism.

As you mature, you won't run through different types as often.

For example:

- ✓ Connor, 13, is rebellious, disconnected, passive-aggressive, and cooperative.
- ✓ Kal, 16, is disconnected, passive-aggressive, & cooperative.
- ✓ Ella, 19, is disconnected and cooperative

Most teens are cooperative at least some of the time. And why not? Cooperation can feel good. It's a nice feeling to get along with people.

It takes a lot of effort and energy to be angry.

WHAT *DOES* DEFIANCE FEEL LIKE?

Take a deep breath and let it out.
Don't worry – nothing too kooky!
Get calm and quiet the mental chatter.

I'm going to ask you some questions and *I want you to feel your answer as a physical sensation, rather than thinking your answer with your intellect.*

Scenario A

Think back to a time when you were being rebellious or felt angry, afraid, or disappointed because of an interaction with an adult in your life. Think about what was going on and why you felt the way you did.

Then when you're ready, answer the following questions (there are no right or wrong answers):

Which adjectives would you use to describe the scene?

How does your body feel when you remember the scene?

Which part of your body feels the worst? Perhaps there's some aching pain or ripples of nausea.

Now take some time to get quiet again before beginning the next exercise.

Scenario B

Think about a time when you were being cooperative, either with a parent or a teacher. Remember what was going on, and why it was easy to be cooperative. Take time to *feel* the scene. Some of you might smile or feel a shiver or a glow.
Then when you're ready, answer the following questions (remember, there are no right or wrong answers):

Which adjectives would you use to describe the scene?

Does remembering the scene make you feel peaceful or happy or more carefree?

What body-feelings do you have when you remember the scene?

Okay, you're probably wondering what the heck this is all about! I don't blame you.

When I do this activity with teens, most of you feel pretty good in cooperative situations. The adult is being nice to you and you feel proud helping to create a happy atmosphere. As I mentioned above, you many find yourself smiling or glowing.

Now go back to Scenario A and notice which part of your body felt bad.
For most people, that part of your body (it's different for different people) can act as a reminder or signal that things aren't as they should be. Sometimes we can't identify how we're feeling until we feel it in our bodies. For instance, when I'm angry, my shoulders and jaw tighten up. When I'm afraid, it's in my gut and my heart.

So this is cool:

You've got the uncomfortable feeling you had being uncooperative, and you've got the happy and proud sensation you had being cooperative. When you are feeling uncomfortable, reach for the happy and proud feeling and "lay" it on top of the uncomfortable feeling. I know it sounds a bit strange, but I also know you can do this. Then you don't have to be controlled by your mirror neurons or your fears!

Try smiling

Even a goofy grin (or *especially* a goofy grin) speeds up the process.

Again, I know. It's nutty. And it works. I promise.

Try it again later today and see what happens. Imagine the tense situation again and then bring your happy feeling to the part of you that feels angry, afraid, or disappointed.

Try it more than once.

I Have a Dream

I think most of you know about Martin Luther King, Junior's famous "I Have a Dream" speech. (If you don't, it's a must-read, and you can easily find it online.) In it, he outlined his wishes for a safer and more peaceful world, where all races could happily co-exist.

One of the things I love best about the speech is that he urged people to not let bitterness block their hearts from creating more unity:

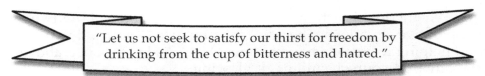

"Let us not seek to satisfy our thirst for freedom by drinking from the cup of bitterness and hatred."

When life (or parents) seems unfair, when we're dying to break free from circumstances that seem to be pushing us down, it's hard not to feel envy and resentment. Martin Luther King, Junior knew how easy it is to be overwhelmed by those feelings. We get a physical "rush" of excitement – sort of a shiver of danger and meanness – and it's hard to resist.

We see others having what we want, getting to do things we want to do, and we want some of that! WE want to feel good also. *Our body turns us to thoughts of revenge, getting even, gossip, and put-downs.*

We all experience it. Some of us have learned to flip our thoughts toward more positive endeavors and, with this book, you can too.

It actually takes more energy to be angry and vengeful than it takes to be loving and accepting.

Don't believe me? I'll prove it to you:

Feel your anger right now. Do you feel how everything is churning inside you? How your body is getting tense? How your senses are on alert?

Now feel loving. Think about a person or pet you just adore. Let that love wash over you. Isn't your body starting to relax? (I see you smiling!) It's like your body is resting now. It's so effortless.

Ta-da! Anger requires more energy than love.

Thank you, thank you. And you're welcome. ☺

I've mentioned before that it's super important, in training your parents, to come from a place of honesty, open-mindedness, and willingness.

You can't expect them to be eager if your tone of voice or your body language (frowning, for instance) says, "Yeah, so you two have pretty much been jerks to me and now I'm going to teach you how to be better parents."

Parents & teens have the power to connect and be happy in their relationships with one another.

Take some time to think:

What is your dream for your family?
How do you want your family to interact?
Less yelling?
More family dinners?
More camping trips?
Less church?
More respect?
More fun?
Fewer chores?
Less teasing?

Write down your Family Dream so you have a record of it that you can't possibly forget. (You do have busy lives. Forgetting happens.)

RETICULAR ACTIVATION, OR HERE'S ANOTHER COOL THING ABOUT YOUR BRAIN AND FOCUSING ON THE GOOD STUFF, AND HOW MUCH POWER YOU HAVE, AND HOW YOU CAN TRAIN YOUR PARENTS IN A WEIRD WAY THAT DOESN'T SEEM LIKE IT MAKES SENSE, BUT IT DOES, AND IT WORKS!

Reticular Activation (that first word is pronounced: reh-TIH-kyu-ler) basically means that we see what we want to see. It's how the brain sorts through the massive amounts of information that come at us all the time. (See the Credits for a great article)

For example, your parents just bought a Maserati. Now, despite the fact that a Maserati is an unusual car to see on the road, you see them every single day. That's reticular activation. You have Maseratis on your mind and your brain responds by showing them to you.

Or, you have a black dog you adore. You haven't really noticed black dogs before, but ever since you got your dog, it seems like they're all over the place. Your brain has been trained to notice black dogs because you love a black dog.

That's reticular activation, and *you can train your brain to notice things you weren't noticing before*. AND, you will also be training your parents at the same time.

I am not kidding.

"What? How? When?" you may be wondering . . .

Remember, Martin Luther King, Junior advised that real change can't happen through anger and resentment. So let's look at your Dream, not your disappointments:

Let's say on your Dream List you put:

✓ I want to fight less with my parents.
✓ I want to have more family nights.
✓ I want my parents to trust me more.
✓ _____ .
✓ _____ .

Okay, so here's what you do:

✓ Every time you avoid a fight with your parents, write it down.

✓ Every time you have a family night, write it down.

✓ Every time your parents show they trust you more, write it down.

✓ Every time _____ , write it down.

Literally. Write down: "My parents trusted me to come home on time." Or, "We had a game night tonight."

Put the date and write down just how your dream is actually coming true!

Honestly, honestly, honestly – if you do this you will see that your parents will fight with you less, you'll have more family nights, and they will trust you more.

It is SO weird, but it works. I do it myself. But you gotta write it down. Keep a log of each time. I have my log on my computer desktop.

One exception: it won't work with anything you're not a part of. For instance, your mother stopping smoking is not in your power. Neither is your father losing weight. Those things are not about you.

When you feel frustrated with your family, go back to your Family Dream, and go back to your log. Also, grab onto some of the other exercises in this book if you're feeling a bit crazy. Try to come from a place of calm and not anger. Talking to an angry person is like talking to a drunk person. Neither of you will understand the other.

You'll find that the more you practice these exercises, the more loving and trusting your family is.

It's purdy cool.

THINKING ABOUT DAY THREE

You've done a lot so far!
In Day Three, we talked about teen stereotypes and, also, the different ways teens try to get attention from adults.

You also learned that you don't have to rebel; you can control your reactions by replacing negative feelings with positive ones (and by "feelings" I mean "physical sensations").
And I threw in some MLK, Jr.
And some scientific awesomeness.

All in all, a packed chapter.

Exercises like soothing your resentments or disappointments, and knowing about Reticular Activation will help you become a much better trainer!
Remember, your parents may be operating – at least a bit – from fear, so they'll probably be a bit defensive. They'll be more likely to listen and to change if you're encouraging rather than bossy.

What was the most helpful thing you learned on Day Three?

What's one thing you learned that you think your best friend would find interesting? How about your siblings? Your parents?

You might want to reward yourself at this point. Give yourself a high-five from me ☺
If you want to take a break to let all this sink in, go ahead. It's absolutely okay to take time off, or to spend some time practicing the exercises I've already given you. Practice makes progress!

If you've made it through the first three days and you're still ready for more, great!
On to Day Four!

DAY FOUR
You're in Charge. Be the Change.

> "I hate how parents expect so much of you, and when you make one mistake, it's like the world is coming to an end." Brittany, 14
>
> "I told them, 'I'm stressing and you need to stop pushing. I'm going to make my own decisions.'" Jeremiah, 16

Families with teens are acting less like families and more like contestants on the TV show *Survivor ™*. I know you know what I'm talking about. Everyone thinks it's their job to "outwit, outplay, and outlast" each other.

Who has the power?
How did they get it?
How can I get it away from them?
I've got some; how do I get more?

You don't have conversations anymore; you have power struggles! It's like a twisted, crazy tug-of-war to see who can hold out longer – the parent or the teen.

There's a saying, "The squeaky wheel get the grease." It means that the more you whine, complain, and make a lot of noise, the quicker people will give you attention. This is a tactic many kids, teens, and even immature adults use. You push and push and push and finally your parents give in because they can't take it anymore.

Another tactic is to throw up a wall of defense. When you feel like your parents are closing in on you, hanging around too much, wanting too much of your time, you throw up a wall to keep them out, like a castle wall keeps out invaders.

Yay! You've defeated the enemy!

But did you win?

You might say, "Yes, I won, because I got what I wanted," but I would strongly disagree.

> You can bug your parents until they give in to your demands, but that's no way to get the respect you want and deserve.

You want respect and love and a sense of belonging and to be valued, and you get none of that when you're a squeaky wheel. All you get is the chance to say that you can yell, complain, and create chaos better than your parents. That's a pretty weird victory, if you ask me.

TIME FOR A NEW STRATEGY

What if you could be victorious *and* lovable? It's possible, but you can't do it just by showing up to the game: you've got to have a strategy.

Imagine a *Survivor* ™ contestant who didn't come in with a good strategy. "The Tribe Has Spoken!"

Imagine a couple in *The Amazing Race* that didn't have some strategy for working together. They'd be stuck in some foreign country!

And if you've watched even one episode of *American Idol*, you've heard a judge comment that a contestant chose a song that didn't fit his or her ability or personality.

Strategies are conscious decisions.

They outline how we want to interact with people, how we want to complete an assignment or project, how we want to play a game or sport, or how we will behave when faced with a life challenge.

> A strategy is a map that can guide you through new territory. And *this* is new territory, my friend.

And this applies to training your parents as well. You've tried to train them without a well-considered strategy. How has *that* worked out?

Imagine training a dog. You can't just force rules on the poor thing. You have to establish a bond. And the way to do that is to get to know your dog a bit. The mistake many owners make is they don't really understand their pet; the owner just thinks about what he or she wants and then assumes that the dog will go along with it.

Or, at the other extreme, owners think their pets need to be beaten to obey. Yikes!

You already know that when parents take one or the other of those approaches they can alienate their children. Nevertheless, some teens also think that either:

✓ My parents will do whatever I want, or
✓ My parents need a good shock to their systems!

If it doesn't work when parents do it, *why would it work when you do it?*

Another strategy that never works is trying to be like someone else. "I'll be like Trey or Bella or Ray and then everything will be fine." Parents do this too. They say, "I'll parent like Mrs. Smith does. Her children are very well-behaved." Never works. And don't you hate it when a parent or teacher says, "Your sister would never do that!" or "Why can't you be more like your brother?"

Perhaps a better question is, "Why can't you be more like *you?*"

FALSE EVIDENCE APPEARING REAL

Before you answer that question, let's look at who you're not.

When we're not ourselves, it's usually because we're afraid that who we are isn't good enough or fun enough or attractive enough. The truth is we're all good enough. I don't even have to meet you to know you're just fine the way you are. Granted, you will grow and change and hopefully become more and more awesome – sooner rather than later – but for now, today, you are just fine.

But there's a monster who lives inside you, preventing you from being everything you could be. Its name is Fear, and it wears costume after costume trying to get the attention that makes it thrive.

Sometimes Fear looks like a test, sometimes it looks like a dentist, sometimes it looks like your parents arguing.

> Fear's best disguise is when it looks and talks just like you.

But Fear's best disguise is when it masquerades as you!

That's right.

All that time you spend putting yourself down, telling yourself you're not good enough, smart enough, pretty enough, talented enough, or successful enough . . .

That's not really you.
That's fear disguised as you.

Fear speaks in a perfectly calm voice or it scolds you in anger, but each time it sounds rational and reasonable.

It's doing such a great imitation of you that you actually believe it *is* you.

And the more you hear it, the more you believe it.

But it's not you.

Think about it:
If Fear looked like a ferocious tiger, you wouldn't get close.
If Fear looked like a zombie, you would know to run away.

The only way fear can live is to trick you into inviting it in, **and whom would you most likely invite in first?**
Yourself – the most familiar person in the world.

You say to yourself:

> It sounds like me, it uses the same vocabulary I use, it seems to know my life history, so it must be me, and it must be telling the truth. I am a loser, a nothing!
>
> Well, at least I know now, so I never have to try to be anything else. Thank God I don't have to waste my life having dreams and trying to reach them. Boy, would that be a waste of my time.

So we become someone else.

We put on the costume of fear.
And nobody knows because we still look the same.

We never hear this voice and think, "Wait, what? That's not me at all!"

And every time our parents say, "You should be getting better grades," you think to yourself, "No, I can't. I'm not that smart."
Or when your parent says, "You're a very pretty girl/handsome young man," you think sarcastically, "Right. That's why I have so many people falling in love with me."

It's Fear that tells the lie that we're not good enough or attractive enough, and then, all our actions from this point on affirm that belief.

When we keep telling ourselves we're not capable and talented, we become less capable and talented.

It's FEAR that tells us we're not good enough. But Fear is often a liar.

So when our parents say we're smarter, kinder, prettier, stronger, or more whatever than we think we are, we either attack or put up that wall. "What do they know? They HAVE to say that. I know it's not true. My parents are lying."

But guess what?

They're the ones who are right!
They're speaking from Love.
You're the one telling yourself lies.
You're speaking from F.E.A.R.

F = False
E = Evidence
A = Appearing
R = Real

Fear (False Evidence Appearing Real) takes control and, without us knowing it, all our decisions become fear-based. We think we're in a competition and our parents are the enemy. We live in fear that they will control us so we act uncontrollable:

✓ I'll never get what I want from my parents, so I'll yell and nag so much that they'll have to give it to me.

✓ My parents keep telling me I'm not reaching my potential. I have no potential and I'll prove it to them by getting bad grades.

✓ It's my parents' fault that I lie. If they'd give me more privileges I wouldn't have to lie about where I am and what I'm doing.

DO YOU REALLY WANT TO FEEL THAT BAD ALL OVER AGAIN?

When we hold onto our fears and mix in some anger and resentment, we get poison.

The word "resentment" comes from Latin. It means, "to feel again." Isn't that true of resentments? They just don't die. We feel that anger and disappointment over and over again.

Remember Martin Luther King, Junior's quote about resentment and bitterness, in Day Three? Here's another quote (anonymous author) on the same topic. Looks like we have a consensus: resentment, jealousy, and bitterness destroy *us* more than they destroy the other person.

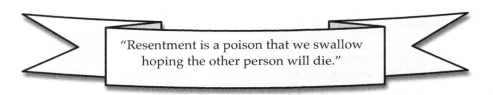

"Resentment is a poison that we swallow hoping the other person will die."

I'm sure you've had the experience of being mad at someone and they couldn't care less. In fact, they may not even know you're mad at them. Doesn't that just make you so mad?!

We get angrier and angrier and they just go about life not having a care in the world.

We poison *our* lives by obsessing over someone who doesn't even notice. Why do we do such a crazy thing?

CONTROL YOURSELF!

Fear and anger and resentment live in the primitive part of our brain. (More on this in the Credits section.) The "Lizard Brain" is concerned with survival. This is the part that used to worry about saber-tooth tigers and poisonous dino-monsters and big spears.

Nowadays, we rarely need this survival center in our brain – I mean, how many saber-tooth tigers hang out in your neighborhood?

It's the same part of the brain that gets activated when we feel threatened, the "fight or flight" response that you've probably heard of.

Some of us fight back when we feel threatened. We're the yellers.

Some of us run away when we feel threatened. We're the wall putter-uppers.

The structure of this part of our brain is so old, passed down through the centuries, that we sometimes say that fear and anger are practically instinctual responses. I *will* say that fear and anger sure do become habits. *You* might even say, "I can't control my body chemistry; the adrenalin rush just happens!"

But you can control it!

✓ **Remember Your Mirror Neurons**. You and your parents act crazy with each other because you're mirroring each other. If one of you stays calm, the other will calm down.

✓ **Learn these Universal Truths** (meaning: they're true for everyone. We'll revisit and explore them more on Day Six.) If you can keep these in mind, your reaction time will slow down so you won't have to freak out so often:

- People who try to control everything really feel out of control.

- People who are angry are just feeling out of control and afraid.

- People who say they don't need any help with anything are terrified that they're losing control.

(See a pattern here? People who get angry and frustrated need our compassion. They're afraid).

✓ **Practice Thought-Flipping**. Even though it appears someone is attacking you or trying to make your life miserable, *unless it's a fact, it's just Fear*. Flip your fearful thoughts and tell yourself something else.

- My parents want the best for me.

- My parents love me.

- I have a good life.

- I can get good grades. I'm smart.

- I get along with my parents.

- _____

- _____

- _____

✓ **Soothe yourself** by talking quietly and gently to yourself. I know it sounds weird and mushy, but this is probably the single most important thing you can do to change your own body chemistry.

✓ **Talk to your fear** as if it were a little child. Tell it that everything's okay, that you're okay, that it's time to relax and breathe slowly. Repeat those words over and over until you calm down. It really can stop you from overreacting.

You are not anger, resentment, and fear, and neither are your parents. Love is the inner voice you can trust.

> You learned to soothe yourself when you were a baby, and you can learn to do it again.

And if it doesn't sound like your voice or like your parents' voices, I'm sure there are adults at your school, community center, or house of worship who speak to you kindly and with genuine interest and caring. Those are the voices of Love. Listen to those voices.

WINNERS TRAIN WINNERS

Now we know what gets in the way of training your parents: letting fear and anger become your strategy.

Then what does it take to become a successful parent-trainer?

Let's pretend you're training or coaching a contestant for a reality show. Let's pretend that when you're done coaching this person, they're going to be a mega-super-colossal winner.

It's easy to think of qualities that would get someone kicked off the show. Let's start there:

Lazy	**Gives up easily**
Doesn't care about winning	**Not willing to take chances**
Untalented	**Has some confidence**
Bored a lot	**High maintenance** (requires a lot of attention)

Someone with those qualities would be eliminated pretty quickly.

Can you imagine someone on *Survivor* ™ insisting that they can only eat gourmet food?
Or someone on *The Amazing Race* sleeping all day long?
Or an *American Idol* winner who sings off-key?
Part of almost any successful strategy would involve being the opposite of the qualities above!

To be successful, you've got to have skills and you've got to be committed to your success. If you really want to win, you can't be casual and not care about what happens.

Now, what about the coach?

A good trainer motivates and inspires.

Coaches don't start with a group of people who know exactly what they're doing. If they knew what they were doing, they wouldn't need a coach. Even the greatest athletes have coaches so they can achieve their personal best.

If you're trying to train or coach someone to win, can you afford to be lazy, uncaring, timid, or whiny? I think not! When a parent calls me and asks for help, I can't sound like Eeyore! I have to inspire them!
When a student yells at me (I work with an interesting group of kids, what can I say?) I can't just start crying or turn around and attack them! I need patience.

Are you catching on?

In order to be a good trainer or coach, you also have to have winning qualities.

And you have to develop *your* winning qualities first, because you're the teacher here. You're the motivator.

And it's the same with training your parents.

You have to *give* the thing that you most want from them.
You have to show them how it's done.

As the Indian spiritual and political leader Mahatma Gandhi famously said:

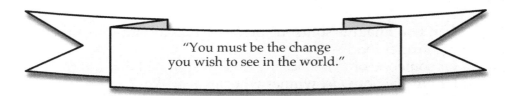

"You must be the change
you wish to see in the world."

If you want your parents to be kind, show them kindness.
If you want them to stop yelling, you stop yelling.
If you want your parents to compliment you, you compliment them first.
Show them, don't tell them. *Be* the change.
That's part of strategizing as well.

So how do you want your parents to behave?

You're doing the training so you can choose which qualities you want to train your parents to have.
(Sweet!)

IT'S BUILD-A-BETTER-PARENT TIME!

First, circle 8 – 10 of the qualities below, and add any that I may have forgotten.
Choose qualities your parents need help with, and that you would **love** your parents to have.

Kind	Protecting
Flexible	Respectful
Relaxed	Successful
Forgiving	Not judgmental
Easy to talk to	Generous
Complimentary	Spends time with you
A team player	Not angry
Affectionate	Doesn't yell
Hard working	Friendly
Nurturing	Honest
Inspiring	Loving
Organized	Accepting
Fun	Has integrity
Clean	Interesting

Notice these are also many of the qualities of a good coach or trainer. Remember that you, as the trainer, have to exhibit these qualities first.

Are you ready?

Okay, next, choose *three* of those ten qualities you circled.

You'll start training yourself first so you can show your parents what their behavior should look like, so choose carefully.

✓ You can choose qualities you already have but want to strengthen.

✓ You can choose qualities you don't yet have but would like to have.

Or,

✓ You can mix it up.

Don't stress about your choices. Once you start, they'll follow your lead. Parents catch on pretty quickly.

Let's revisit Isaac, the one whose father called him a "Mama's Boy."

Isaac decided that he wanted his parents to be more **Relaxed, Forgiving, and Respectful.**

Of course, this meant that he, also, had to be relaxed, forgiving, and respectful. It wasn't as easy as he thought it would be, but we worked out an awesome strategy for getting what he wanted:

Isaac didn't have to go all out and try to do everything at once, he could learn one quality at a time.

First, Isaac realized that his parents were nicer and more relaxed when his room was clean, so what do you think he did? He cleaned his room more often. So simple. And so powerful. He just did something that would make them happy and they were happy. Kind of a DUH moment, in some ways, but not so obvious when parents and teens are fighting.

Second, Isaac decided that he needed to show his parents how to be forgiving. Every time his parents made a mistake and were apologetic ("Oops, sorry about that" was good enough for Isaac) he would reply, "That's okay. Human error." This took a bit more work because he didn't really want to forgive his parents. But he did want them to be more forgiving towards him, so . . . As it turns out, they loved all his forgiving and started repeating the phrase themselves.

Third, when one of Isaac's parents seemed about to start lecturing him, Isaac would ask, "When you're finished, can I have a chance to talk?" This was the most challenging because 1) Isaac had a habit of interrupting, and 2) Isaac thought that all his parents wanted was to blame him and tell him all the things he was doing that were wrong. Sitting through that was rather excruciating.

This last one took the longest. He and his parents had developed a habit that when Isaac was out of line, even a bit, his parents would get scared and frustrated. Then they would lecture him, and Isaac would end up feeling like they thought he was a stupid jerk (again) and he would interrupt them to defend himself. And on and on. It was really just a bunch of Fear.

YOUR TURN!

You're going to list the three qualities you're going to work with, and then pick some actions you can try out.

Planning ahead is also part of good strategizing. You don't have to actually do all these actions – just one per category – but it's a good idea to have options.

Sometimes, for some reason, your "Plan B" becomes the best plan, and you may decide to go with that instead of "Plan A."

Let's start with the first quality you want your parents to have:

Quality _____

Action 1 _____

Action 2 _____

Action 3 _____

Now, what are two other qualities you want your parents to have? What are you willing to go through to train them?

Don't pick something you won't follow through on, because you won't see any results - things will just stay the same.

On the other hand, challenging yourself can be a good thing too. The more you're willing to stretch yourself, the greater the progress you'll make in training your parents.

Quality _____

Action 1 _____

Action 2 _____

Action 3 _____

Quality _____

Action 1 _____

Action 2 _____

Action 3 _____

THINKING ABOUT DAY FOUR

In Day Four we talked about the problem with family power struggles, how Fear makes us less than we are, how to control our fear, and how to be a kick-butt parent trainer!

If you've come this far, you have done a ton. I bet you're beginning to see changes already.

What was the first change you noticed?

What is the *best* change you've noticed so far?

Have your parents noticed any good changes? What have they said?

Some of you may not notice any changes yet. That's okay. Don't worry. If you're feeling overwhelmed, you might want to:

✓ Take a break and come back to this chapter.
✓ Do some writing on the questions below.
✓ Peek at the ½ Day chapter, which is about resisting change.
✓ Peek at Days Five and Six.
✓ Re-read some of the previous chapters.
✓ Call a friend to talk about what you're learning from this book.
✓ Take a nap!

What part of Day Four is still confusing?

What part of Day Four is a bit scary?

What part would you like to discuss with a friend or relative?

Whatever you decide to do next, it's all good. You rock. You really do.

½ DAY
Excuses, Excuses!

> "I don't want to be the one to change. Why can't my parents change? They're the problem!" Brooke, 14
>
> "I'm trying to change but it's not working." Ethan, 16

A RIDDLE ABOUT FROGS*

Question:
Three frogs sat in a pond on their lily pads. One decided to jump in. How many frogs were left sitting on their lily pads?

Answer:
Three.
Why? Because that one frog only made a decision. *He didn't actually jump in!*

GOT RESISTANCE?

I've talked about resistance before, and at this point in your journey to train your parents, you may be thinking,

"None of this is going to work. Be the change? That's not fair!"

You're right: it's not fair. I agree.
What would be fair is if we got an instruction manual when we were born. It would tell us how to act and what to say so we would never make mistakes and never be uncomfortable.
But that's not reality. And I can tell you from much experience, when we fight reality we lose every time!

Excuses and resistance urge us to live a small life. Resistance likes to find fault with everything so that it can go back to being comfortable.

We create excuses and we resist because it's scary to be as wonderful as we were meant to be.

Author and speaker, Marianne Williamson wrote:

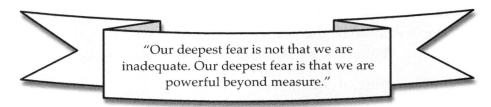

"Our deepest fear is not that we are inadequate. Our deepest fear is that we are powerful beyond measure."

Your parents may be resisting now as well.

If it seems like they're "see-sawing" back and forth between wanting to change and wanting to control you, that's resistance.

If it seems like they're trying to stop you from changing, that's called "push back."

They know in their hearts that family life will be more harmonious if they stop fighting, but fear tells them that love is too wishy-washy, and that it can't solve a serious problem.

And what if they let themselves change and it turns out all this doesn't really work? Then they have to do more work to change back and maybe the family will be in worse shape than before.

And on and on . . .

They too fear their greatness.

Resistance is totally natural. In fact, I'd say it's a good thing. It means we're on the edge of a fantastic breakthrough, if we keep moving forward.

Resistance is all part of moving forward. Between deciding to make a change and actually making that change, there's a big Fear Monster, trying to keep you scared and small.

So what are you going to do?

The truth is, you don't have to change. You can stop here. *But are you making this decision out of fear and doubt, or out of love and self-worth?*

Before you decide, look at this list of excuses that fear and resistance use to convince you to give up your curiosity, your plans, your dreams, and your goals.

See if you've had any of these thoughts while working through this book.

Check off the ones that sound familiar:

❐ "I'm too busy! I really can't fit this into my day."

❐ "I'll do this later. It can wait."

❐ "If I do these exercises, something bad will happen."

❐ "I can't find the book. I can't find a pen or pencil to use."

❐ "I can't concentrate. I'm falling asleep."

❐ "This takes way too long!"

❐ "My friend thinks this is stupid, so it probably is."

❐ "This is too hard. There's no way I can do this by myself."

❐ "My parents will grow out of this phase." (☺)

❐ "I've tried everything. This won't work either."

❐ "I broke my arm and can't turn the pages."

❐ "The dog ate my book/pencil/contacts/whatever."

BAD DECISIONS AND GOOD DECISIONS

When we make a decision because what's in front of us is too scary, it's often the wrong decision. We make lots of bad decisions because we're afraid to fail, we're afraid of what others will think of us, or because we don't feel we're deserving of good things.

What are some bad decisions you've made out of fear? I'll start with some examples from teens I know and love:

✓ Stella stopped eating because she felt more alert and could concentrate on her homework better and, thus, get better grades.

✓ Kal stole a video game controller so he could play when his parents were asleep. They found it, took it from him, and he stole another one.

✓ Max ran away from home so he wouldn't have to give his mom his report card.

✓ Georgia isn't very good at P.E. so she tries to get kicked out of class as much as possible.

You can see how we get stuck when we're afraid. We make the same mistakes over and over, plus add new ones!

What bad decisions have you made because you were afraid? You can list some here, if you'd like.

A good decision is sometimes hard to figure out. Making decisions is about taking chances, and that's scary. And sometimes "good" decisions don't feel great because Fear is doing its best to interfere.

A good decision, though, nurtures your self-worth. Not the part of you people see, but the real you, under the public person you show to others. A good decision often turns you into a better person. You might ask yourself, "Will my decision benefit other people, or will it just make me feel less afraid for now?"

When making decisions, it's good to have a trusted adult to help us.

Sometimes people won't like your good decisions and this is where it's good to ask a trustworthy adult for help before making your decision (remember the essay in the back of the book about finding trustworthy adults).

Let's revisit one of the bad decisions above, applying the good decision suggestions:

Stella made the decision to be more alert so she could get more schoolwork done. On the surface, this seems like a good decision, and she felt good about it. Eating, in her opinion, would make her feel less alert and that would feel bad.

But Stella put her self-image, her reputation (good student) before her self-worth (her health). We all deserve and need our good health. It's hard to help others when we're too sick to help ourselves.

Because health problems don't always show up immediately, people tend to ignore health *maintenance* until an illness or other problem asserts itself aggressively.

The truth is that starving yourself starves your brain as well, which is the opposite of what Stella was trying to achieve in the first place!

You can see why the "right" decision is confusing at times, and may be a bit scary. Doing the right thing isn't always the same as doing the *easy* thing.

Here are some examples:

✓ Marcus decided to tell his parents he had a boyfriend. He was very nervous that his parents would be judgmental and angry. Instead, they gave Marcus money so he and his friend could go out for coffee.

✓ Will joined the Junior Varsity tennis team, even though he was afraid. He had never been on a team and wasn't sure that he was that great at playing tennis. He didn't want to be teased by his teammates. He did so well though (with help from his teammates) that next year he'll be on the Varsity team.

✓ Mari, a smart and friendly girl, found herself crying a lot and she didn't know why. Her grades were dropping and life didn't make sense. She told her parents she needed help. She thought her parents would tell her she was being a baby. Instead, they thanked her for telling them and made a doctor's appointment for that week. Everyone was relieved.

✓ Georgia (the girl who got kicked out of P.E.) came to talk to me about her class. Together, we figured out that getting kicked out made her feel better for about 20 minutes but then she felt foolish and ashamed. She decided those 20 minutes weren't worth it, and that she was messing up her long-term goals (going to college to become a lawyer). We made a plan that she and I would connect right before P.E. so she could be reminded of her goals.

So what good decisions have you made?

Let's not forget the frogs on the lily pad.
Making a decision is not enough.
It must be followed by action or it means little.
Deciding to dive into the pond is a good first step, but it won't get you results until you actually take the plunge.

If you're still afraid, that's okay. Fear happens.
Ignoring it doesn't work.

Getting it on paper does.
Write about what else you're afraid of.
Keep going.
Write and write and write.
Get mad if you need to. Just get out whatever is keeping you resistant to change.

When you're ready to take that plunge, I'll walk with you, just as I have throughout this book. We'll go at your pace.
Just promise yourself that, to the best of your ability, one minute at a time, you will let love, not fear, guide you.

And, yes, I still mean it – this absolutely will work!

---

* I don't have a thing for frogs. It's totally a coincidence that there are two frog stories in this book. I actually like dogs and tigers and birds. Notice that there are dogs and tigers in this book. I'm sorry there are no birds.

DAY FIVE
Change Your View, Change Your Expectations

> "My mom always says, 'I don't want you to make the same mistakes that I did.' I don't want to make her mistakes either!"
> Catalina, 16
>
> "I hate how my dad and mom never want better for themselves."
> Priya, 16

"BE CAREFUL HOW YOU INTERPRET THE WORLD: IT IS LIKE THAT."
ERICH HELLER

Imagine yourself with an old pair of glasses: you're stylin' some dirty masking tape to hold the two sides together (these are O-L-D glasses). The lenses are smudged and cracked. You look kinda crazy wearing them, but you can't tell because you've gotten used to them. You think they work just fine, you think you can see everything clearly. But you've created a reality based on your unfocused view of the world, a world often colored by feelings of anger, fear, and frustration (our old "friends").

It feels like we're powerless, it feels like the world is a mess, but it's our perception that's a mess. Anger, frustration and fear have blurred our vision, making us think that life is chaotic and random, but this isn't true. We have power. We just need a different pair of glasses.

If Erich Heller (above) is right, if we change our thoughts about the world, our experiences will change too! Change your view, and you change your experience.
It's time for an "eyeball overhaul."

What does this have to do with parenting? Well, to be blunt: the thoughts and judgments you have about your parents may not, in fact, reflect the reality of the situation.

Translation: you're making stuff up about your parents and telling it to other people, and a bunch of it isn't true. It's just your perception and you created your perception!

Now parents do this as well, as I'm sure you are aware. They come to me and tell me that if their children don't get better grades, they will end up working at fast-food restaurants for the rest of their lives.

But that's fear and confusion fogging up *their* glasses.

Just like your parents need to see the reality of who you really are, today, right in front of them, you've got to interact with the parents you have, right now, today, not the ones you wish you had!

Question: What are these made-up things called?
Answer: Assumptions.

ASSUMPTIONS DISTORT REALITY

Assumptions aren't reality, and when it turns out they're true, then they're not assumptions anymore. Until they're proven true, however, they're just judgments we create so we can give some sort of meaning to a situation or so we can label a person we're dealing with.

Assumptions are actually fiction, pretending to be reality. And assumptions can really do a number on our relationships.

So, for today, Day Five, you're going to *smash* those assumptions into itty-bitty pieces.

Even seemingly obvious assumptions – ones that make perfect sense – may not be real, depending on the situation.

Let's look at some really basic examples:

✓ When it rains, I assume I ought to wear a rain parka. But what if it's also sunny and warm?

✓ When I'm tired, I assume I'm sleeping too little. But sleeping too much can make me tired as well.

✓ When I've paid someone money to do a particular job, I assume that it will be done well. But what if that person is unethical?

SMASH Assumptions! They keep us ignorant.

✓ When I'm low on gasoline, I assume I should buy more as soon as possible but what if I need the money for food or medicine?

See what I mean?

What assumptions have you made from time to time, that may not be accurate?

For instance, what assumptions have you made about your favorite teacher, that you're not sure are true?

What assumptions have you made about your *least* favorite teacher, that you're not sure are true?

Here are some more. Fill in the blanks:

"I assume if _____ , then _____ .
But I don't know for sure."

"I assume when _____ , then _____ .
But I don't know for sure."

Here are assumptions that kids might make:

✓ If my parents are married, they must be in love with each
   other.
✓ If my father smokes cigarettes, they must be safe.
✓ If my parents really loved me, they wouldn't yell at me.
✓ My brother/sister gets better grades, so my parents must
   love him/her more than they love me.

You know that these assumptions are pretty much false.

BACK TO ~~PREHISTORIC TIMES~~ YOUR PARENTS' CHILDHOODS

Parents often tell me they love to think back to when their
children were little. It reminds them of how precious you are and how
much you are loved. It takes the focus off the confusing and
frustrating parts of parenthood.
   What if you could have a similar memory of your parents?
What if you could take the focus off the confusing and frustrating
parts of their parenting?

Picturing our parents as children reminds us that they, too, deserve care and love.

What if you imagined
your parents as toddlers or grade
school students or teens?

   Would they be precious or
precocious? Free or feisty?
Approachable or angry? Or all of the
above?

Let's go back in time:

For the first part of the exercise, you're going to look at the
chart below and then...

Write T for True
Write F for False
Check FACT if you know this is absolutely true
Check GUESS if you assume your answer is correct but you're not sure.

If the answer is T for one parent and F for another, you can mark both. You just gotta keep it all straight in your head.

Notice whether you're sure about the answer because you've heard a parent tell you the answer, or whether you think you know the answer based on other information (that would be an assumption!)

What assumptions do you have about your parents as children and teens?	T/F	FACT	GUESS
My parents were healthy babies.			
My parents were well-behaved toddlers.			
My parents were happy toddlers.			
Nothing bad happened to my parents as children.			
My parents had lots of friends when they were kids.			
My parents were happy teenagers.			
My parents were popular as teens.			
My parents had healthy romances in high school.			
As teens, my parents got along with their parents.			

For the second part of this exercise, you're going to check your answers with your parents.

You're actually going to talk with them!

I know this is the first time in this book that I'm asking you to really interact with your parents. I'm going to make it as easy as possible. You don't have to do it right this second if you don't want to; you can just rehearse your interaction.

It can be helpful to look in the mirror and practice so you can notice what your body language is (more about that on Day Six). You can also just sit on your bed and listen to what your voice sounds like when you (pretend) talk to your parents.

But if you want to try it out, I'm going to give you some exercises to get you in the right frame of mind, and then I'm going to give you some scripts you can use, depending on what type of parent you have.

PREPARATION

Practice makes Progress!

✓ **Belly Breathing**. Belly breathing will get you through just about any scary situation. Usually when we're scared or nervous, our breathing is shallow; we don't take in much air. This makes us even more nervous. With belly breathing, you take in a big, slow breath and make your belly stick out. If you can't tell if you're doing it right, put your hand on your stomach and make it rise with your breath. When you exhale, blow it out slowly so that your stomach goes in. Try to breathe out so much that your belly can almost touch your spine. This should be relaxing, so go slowly. Do it 10 times or until you feel calmer.

✓ **Try some writing** if you're still nervous. Write down your fears. Get them out of your brain and onto paper.

✓ **Talk to your fear** and tell it to take some time off. Tell it that it can come back later, but that it can't be here right now.

✓ **Make a list** of all of your parents' good qualities, and then repeat those to yourself. For example:

- My mother has a good sense of humor.
- My mother is smart.
- My mother loves me.
- My father is patient when I seriously need him.
- My father loves me.
- My father bought me this book so he wants to help out!

✓ **Do some Thought-Flipping**. Instead of telling yourself this is going to be difficult and unsuccessful, tell yourself:

- Everything will be fine.
- I can do this with ease and comfort.
- My parents want to connect with me.
- I am calm and happy.
- I am smart and strong.

✓ **Remember your mirror neurons**. If you tell yourself this is a scary, risky, sure-to-fail plan then that's what your parents will pick up from you. Keep it smooth and easy and that's what they'll pick up on!

✓ **Spend more time with the information from Days One – Four**, if you're not feeling ready. That's totally acceptable. There's no reason to speed up if you're feeling shaky. Just don't give up entirely.

Keep in mind it's also important to know when it's a good time to ask questions. For instance, a lot of parents don't like their TV watching to be interrupted. Or their bathroom time.

Timing is Everything!

For some parents, asking questions while they're driving is perfect; for others it's not a good idea at all. Some like to chat at the dinner table. Some parents come home from work all ready to spend time with you; some like a little alone-time to de-stress from the workday. Some like to talk when you help with chores and that might be a good way to approach them.

When are your parents typically in a good mood? Make a list.

When are super-bad times to talk?

When your parents are angry, don't try to have a conversation, and definitely don't push and nag and whine. You will just create more anger.

When are your parents typically in a bad mood? Make a list.

SCRIPTS

Note: it's actually not that important for you to get accurate answers from your parents. What's important is for you to connect without getting into an argument.

If your parent is a Disciplinarian, you want to pay attention to the timing. Interrupting is a bad idea. Get them when they're calm. Also it's a good idea to prepare them. You might say, "Mom? Dad? I answered a questionnaire in my book about parents and I'd like to check my answers with you when you have time." That way, you're not taking time when they feel rushed. It shows respect and caring curiosity too!

You can show your parents the book and say, "I'm learning not to make assumptions. Did I guess these correctly? Can you tell me what the right answers are?"

This is a mature approach and the Disciplinarian will appreciate it because you're looking for facts and accuracy.

If you have Distracted Parents, it would be good to talk to them when they're away from big distractions like technology. Technology takes a lot of attention.

Distracted parents can often pay attention to you better when they're in nature. It can be a quiet garden, a forest, a beach, or even strolling through a zoo, with all the plants and animals.

Think about your parents' comfort.

Also, it's probably better to talk when you're both sitting down instead of when you're walking or your parent is driving or riding a bike. Sitting is very "anchoring" or supportive for distracted people, especially if you're actually on the ground.

Then just say, "I've been reading this book and it asked some easy True/False questions about our parents. Is it okay to check my answers with you now?" If they want to add anything, they will.

It's really hard to make a mistake with a Permissive Parent. You just need to catch them at a time when they're not off doing their own thing. "Hey, I'm reading a great book about parents and kids and it asked us to get some basic facts about our parents' childhoods. Can I go over them with you now?"

Permissive parents are permissive because they're afraid to lose your connection. So if you're asking questions, most of them would feel great!

Talking with even-handed parents is also relatively comfortable. Just choose a time when your parents can give you their attention, and you can take them right through the questionnaire. Easy Peasy.

Quite a few Disconnected Parents aren't unreasonable and unavailable all the time (take Diana, for instance). Sometimes they have the presence of mind to listen to you. Growing up with a Disconnected parent, you've seen that they have two sides. Much like the book, *The Strange Case of Dr. Jekyll and Mr. Hyde,* you probably have a sense of when they're more Dr. Jekyll (the calm one) or more Mr. Hyde (the crazy one). Here are some hints for better communication with your Disconnected parent:

- ✓ Catch them when they're calm, but not tired; coherent (you can understand them), but not distracted.
- ✓ Ask them if they have some time to talk to you now.
- ✓ Say something like, "When you want to stop, just let me know."
- ✓ Ask one question at a time. If things go well, you can add a question.
- ✓ If they say they can't talk now but they'll talk to you later, say "Okay" but don't count on it. They might not be in the mood when that time comes around. It's okay. Another time will come around. Take it nice and easy or, as some of my friends say, "light and polite."
- ✓ Don't try this when they're drunk, high, depressed, anxious, manic, angry, hungry, sad, or tired. Not only won't you get a good answer but you won't connect well either. Trust me on this.

WHAT IF YOU'RE NOT READY?

If you're not comfortable approaching your parents yet, set up some kind of reminder on a calendar, on your cell phone, or just on a piece of paper that you post somewhere. That way you'll remember to ask them when you're more comfortable.

> Light and Polite works for any interaction with your parents, no matter what type.

If *they're* not comfortable, that's okay. Some people are very private, some people are shy, some people didn't have a happy past and don't want to think about it much, and some people are just afraid. Tell them it's okay if they don't want to answer the questions. They'll like hearing that. (Cutting your parents some slack is also part of the training, so really, it's okay if you don't get all your questions answered.)

So? How did it go?

What did they tell you that surprised you the most?

What made you feel closer to your parents or stepparents?

Assumptions can get us into trouble. Perhaps you've heard the expression, "To ASSUME is to make an ASS out of U and ME." (It's a bit naughty, but it helps me remember not to make assumptions!)

In a lot of little ways, we jump to wrong conclusions about our parents every single day. Can you imagine how you would feel if someone jumped to wrong conclusions about you?

Or, a better question might be: how *do* you feel when your parents jump to wrong conclusions, or they make assumptions about you? I know I can't stand when people judge me and, yet, how often do I judge others?

How often do you judge other people?

HOW WE WERE PARENTED AFFECTS HOW WE PARENT

Marcus is the son of Judy and Walt.

One day, Judy called me, because Walt was teasing Marcus about being short. Marcus asked his father to stop, but Walt kept going.

I talked with Walt and asked him to describe his own father. Walt described a disconnected parent, a drunk who was physically violent.

How could Walt know how to be a good father to Marcus when he didn't have a good father-figure of his own?

I know that's a pretty heavy story – all psychological and such – but I believe that when we know who our parents were as kids, we can see how and why they turned out the way they did, and gain some understanding and tenderness for them.

How many of us make assumptions and then make decisions about how we're going to treat someone, when we don't have all the information we need?

Parenting is hard work. And what if you've got some other pain in your life to deal with? What if you're a parent who was hurt by your own parents or by adults close to you? That's gotta hurt, even if it wasn't done on purpose. You know that.
How much harder would it be to parent well?

You just never know how someone's past affects his or her present, but it always does, in one way or another.

COLLECTING MORE INFO ABOUT YOUR PARENTS

Have you ever thought about what other people think of your parents? I mean, not as parents, but as regular adults living their regular adult lives.
What do their friends think?
How about their business colleagues or the people at their house of worship?
Or their own sisters and brothers and cousins?
Or their parents?

Who are your parents? (Besides being your parents, I mean).

It's time to learn some facts about your parents, don't you think? No more assumptions.

You're going to go on a type of scavenger hunt, collecting "memories" from your parents' lives. My hope is that you will gain some understanding that you didn't have before. It doesn't have to make your heart go all mushy. You don't have to run to the front door, open it and shout at the top of your lungs, "I love my parents!"
You don't even have to smile at them.
You just need good old Honesty, Open-mindedness, and Willingness.

SCAVENGER HUNT, Y'ALL!

- ✓ First, tell your parents about this activity, and ask if they would help you with it. If not, that's okay. You'll be able to do some of it, and that's just fine.

- ✓ Find a nice, sturdy box or bag ("Sturdy" here means: not chewed up, ripped, dirty, smelly, stained, smashed, or otherwise raggedy. This is important. Make it nice, people!)

- ✓ Put each item you collect into your sturdy box or bag.

  You will be saving this. Trust me. When you get older, you will be really glad you have this keepsake.

- ✓ Email, text, IM, or FB your mother's mother, father, sister, brother, and childhood friends (whomever you can) and

  1. Ask them to tell you what they most admired about your mom when she was a teenager.

  2. Now ask what bugged them most!

  3. Ask them to tell you about some adventure they shared when they were teens.

  4. See if you can find (or ask for) an old report card or some schoolwork belonging to your mother.

  5. Find (or ask for) a photo of your mother as a baby or young child. Make a copy for yourself, and put back the original.

  6. Find (or ask for) a photo of your mother as a teenager. Make a copy for yourself, and put back the original.

  7. Find (or ask for) one or two other "keepsake" items – an old birthday card or holiday card, a favorite children's book, a drawing, a poem, a toy or stuffed animal, an inexpensive piece of jewelry, some sports item, or some other piece of memorabilia. No stealing!

When you're done, gather all the items and print out the emails, texts, or messages you received and put them in your sturdy bag or box.

If you get into a conversation with your parent(s) while doing this activity – Great!

Now do the same step for your father or stepparents.

When you're done, use the scripts from earlier in the chapter to ask your parents if they would be willing to talk to you about one or two of the items in your box or bag.

Again, if they don't want to talk or they were unwilling to participate, it's okay. Some parents may want to talk about all the stuff. The "sneaky" thing is that you've made it very safe – you're not asking about *them*; you're asking about *the items*, so it will make the conversation a little less scary for everyone.

Make it a habit to look at these items once every month or so. It will give you a warm-hearted feeling that's super important to have while you train you parents to be proper adults ☺

Which items made you laugh?

Did any items(s) make you feel sad? Do you know why?

Which item(s) made you feel some tenderness towards your parents?

Which items are your favorites?

What did you learn about your parents or stepparents that surprised you? Why did it surprise you?

What did you learn about yourself that surprised you? Why did it surprise you?

THINKING ABOUT DAY FIVE

Today was a jam-packed day.

I hope you do something to reward yourself for a job well done!

Today we talked about some important and emotional things like how assumptions can really hurt our relationships with our family and friends.

On the lighter side, you've started to learn how best to talk to your parents, and you got to learn some fun facts from their childhoods as well.

What part of Day Five made you feel really good?

What part of Day Five made you feel a bit anxious, or even a bit angry? Do you know why?

If you haven't done the Day Five exercises yet, take some time to figure out what you might need or what might need to happen for you to feel ready? (Always good to have a strategy!)

I know we don't know each other, and I know this might be hard to believe, but I'm just so proud of you! If you've made it this far in the book, that's HUGE.

"A" for effort!

DAY SIX
No More Power Struggles: You Talk, Your Parents Listen!

> "My mother says I interrupt her all the time,
> but she interrupts *me* all the time" Nate, 11½
>
> "Why do I have to explain everything over and over again?
> Why do I have to explain anything at all?
> I leave for college in a year, and I want some privacy!" Jen, 17

You've arrived at Day Six. Congratulations on making it this far. We've covered a whole lot of ground, and you've had to look at some pretty deep topics: why parents may disconnect from you, what parents fear, what teens fear, and what teens do to get attention.

You've also started to have some good conversations with your parents.

In Day Six we'll focus on how to have serious conversations without freaking out. You will become a powerful communicator with skills to help you throughout your long life.

The stuff I'm sharing with you is totally doable and totally works.
Crazy, yes. Crazy AWESOME!

I suggest you read and do the exercises carefully so you don't miss out on the treasure than can come from having a solid, loving, respectful relationship with your parents.

For fun, let's start with what goes wrong with communication.

TOP 5 COMMUNICATION BLUNDERS PARENTS MAKE

- ✓ They don't really listen. They only let you talk because it's the polite thing to do
- ✓ They make "Killer Statements."
    - "Stop being lazy!"
    - "You're killing me!"
    - "NO ONE in their right mind would do something like that!"
- ✓ They're dishonest. They say one thing, but do another.
- ✓ They use conversation as a way to control you, not to connect with you.
- ✓ They ambush you with new ideas. They don't prepare you for the conversation or let you think about the discussion topic ahead of time.

Feel free to add some of your own!

TOP 5 COMMUNICATION BLUNDERS TEENS MAKE

- ✓ Teens don't really listen. They pretend to listen because that's what's expected of them.
- ✓ Teens make "Killer Statements."
    - "I hate you!"
    - "You can't make me!"
    - "As soon as I turn 18, I'm outta here!"
- ✓ Teens are dishonest. They say one thing, but do another.
- ✓ Teens use talk to control their parents not to connect with them.
- ✓ Teens ambush parents with new ideas, plans, demands, and then expect them to come up with an immediate response.

Your turn! Think you can add to this list?

If you're as smart as I think you are, you've noticed that the blunders that parents make, teens also make. That makes sense to me. After all, who taught you teens to communicate in the first place? Your parents, of course. So if they're fairly ineffective communicators, it's not surprising that you might be too.

This is also really, really good news! It means you can relate really, really well to your parents, and that's key to training them.

On Day Four, we spent a lot of time talking about fear and how, often, it controls us without our being aware of it. F.E.A.R., remember, stands for False Evidence Appearing Real, and this is true in our conversations as well.

Also if you go back to Day Four, you will recall I spoke of Universal Truths about power and feelings of powerlessness. We lie, talk loudly, make demands, insult people, act disrespectfully and unreasonably, and even go silent all because we're afraid that we're not good enough, that nobody truly understands us, or that someone is trying to steal our power.

Let me tell you about some young people I know and like:

Mari **lies** because she's ashamed of her behavior. We lie to cover up mistakes that we're ashamed of, or because we don't think we measure up in some way.

Gabe **yells** because he thinks that's the way to get people to understand him. We talk loudly to get attention. We also talk loudly when we feel out of control.

Catalina **whines** to wear down her parents so she'll get her way. We make demands to show people who's boss.

Truong **insults people** when he wants to feel like he's better than someone else. We insult people to try to take away their power and deflate their sense of self-worth.

Makayla **disrespects** teachers and other authority figures because she thinks they're not safe people. We act disrespectfully and unreasonably because we are terrified that people don't really see us.

Kal **looks down or away** when he talks because he's overwhelmed by life. When we clam up, turn away, or shut down, we think we can control our world by not standing out.

Maybe some of these sound familiar?

In my roles as teacher, school counselor, and family coach, I have had many opportunities to actually see teens and parents move from over-confidence to fear to angry outburst in a matter of seconds.

You hear something that's not what you wanted to hear – a surprising statement or a disappointing response to your question – and you get this wide-eyed look of shock.

> Bad communication skills can quickly turn an innocent conversation into World War 3.

The first thought that comes to you (teens and parents) is "This is wrong. I have to fix it NOW!" And then you're talking back, arguing, making faces, rolling your eyes, mumbling to a friend or to yourself, and making noises that show outrage or disgust. (We all do it, to varying degrees. I just see it more with teens and parents.)

In seconds, fear can turn a reasonable statement into an argument, and then the mirror neurons activate and everybody's caught up in a stressful, disempowering situation.
No one wins.

And that's part of the issue – the whole contest thing; we think that, even in communicating, one person has to win and one has to lose.

I bet you can remember a recent time when you tried to have a conversation with your parent(s) and it turned into a battle. Let's work this through (use your journal or the pages in the back):

What happened?

How did your parent's fear show itself?

How did your fear show itself?

What was the sentence or phrase that triggered the fear?

WHAT DO CONVERSATIONS HAVE TO DO WITH TRAINING YOUR PARENTS?

The #1 reason teens and parents don't get along is that they don't understand one another and they don't know how to talk about not understanding one another.

Everyone goes straight to Judgment, Anger, and Fear. Assumptions fly, voices get louder, and communication breaks down.

Talk about training! If you improve your communication, your parents will be floating on a cloud, they'll be so thrilled!

No one likes to feel ignored. Even if it's not intentional, even if it's because you're nervous, parents tend to think that if you're not conversing with them, you don't care about them. And then they get all weird and start trying to control the situation so they'll feel better.

How do you get your connection back on track? By restoring the lines of communication! If you can talk and listen to your parents, you will become like magical unicorns to them!

A teen that willingly communicates with his or her parents? Impossible!

But when you show them your skills, they will be beyond delighted. They will be ecstatic.

They'll stop nagging and yelling and you'll be able to get what you want. But, keep in mind I'm not thinking small. I'm not thinking cell phones, a car, your own room, a later curfew (although you may get those too).

When I say this book will help you get what you want, I'm talking about more respect, more trust, and more joy. I'm talking about the big time here!

Are you ready for a bigger (and much better) life??

The skills you learn in this chapter will last you a lifetime. You'll strengthen every relationship you ever have!

So I'm going to give you even more tips, tricks, tools, scripts and strategies to really super-charge your communication style and improve your relationship with your parents.

SIX WAYS PEOPLE COMMUNICATE

We're going to start by looking at six ways that people communicate, and we're going to look at how people miscommunicate six ways as well:

Comments vs. Insults

Opinions vs. Being Right

Questions vs. Demands

Honesty vs. Lying

Listening vs. Hearing

Conversations vs. Power Struggles

As we go through these, I'd like you to keep this question in mind: "What's my part in all this?"

Every relationship has 2 people with 2 personalities. It's always good to ask: "What's my part in our conflict?"

In every relationship there are two people. *You're not responsible for their actions but you are responsible for yours.* Much of the tension between teens and their parents is just about fear. So instead of blaming them, take an honest look to figure out your part in creating an unpleasant situation and an unpleasant outcome.

Let's look at this situation with Jeremiah ("Jem") and his dad:

> Jem was out with a friend and was late getting home. His dad texted him, "Don't you remember you were supposed to be home by 4pm?"
>
> Jem texted back, "Don't you remember I told you I'd be home by 5pm?"

Uh-oh. You know what's coming, but why did it have to happen?

Dad was afraid he wasn't getting enough respect and Jem was afraid of being controlled by his dad.

Now I'll be straight with you: Dad could have phrased his text differently. That "Don't you remember" part makes it sound like Jeremiah is an idiot.

But what was Jeremiah's part? He did try to negotiate a later time, but when his father said, "No," Jem ignored him.

When we communicate quickly, when we communicate incompletely, our message is incomplete as well. How, then, can we expect people to respond the way we would hope?

The busier our world, the less time people take to communicate thoroughly. Instead of talking, we email. Instead of emailing, we text. It's taking fewer words to send a message but the human connection is getting lost in all the rushing around.

> When we take time to communicate carefully we're more likely to be understood.

For a message to be communicated, for there to be a human connection, we need to slow down and communicate more carefully. When we can communicate with more thought and more care, we can get across the meaning we want and we can communicate more authentically. When we're not authentic, when we're not our true selves, but simply a sketch or virtual version, we are in a sense being dishonest.

We need to be authentic, real, and honest about our communication so we can be heard the way we want and need to be.

In that way, it's possible for both sides to "win."

COMMENTS VS. INSULTS

Comments are harmless. A comment expresses something you've noticed or something you're thinking. Comments can be facts, ideas, opinions, and/or reactions.

There is nothing about a comment that is negative until we make it so.

What turns a comment into an insult is when you say what's on your mind without regard for the other person's feelings. Killer statements are examples of extreme insults. And, not surprisingly, killer statements are all about fear. Let's look at a couple of killer statements; first from a parent and then from a teen:

"No one in their right mind would do something like that!" really means, "I don't know what I'm doing as a parent. I don't know what to do to be a better parent. I must be a bad parent. What if we never get along ever again? How embarrassing. How sad. How will I live with myself if I can't even get along with my own child?"

Amazing, isn't it, that such a short angry statement could have so much hidden meaning?

Here's the teen one:

"I hate you!" really means, "I feel so frustrated and so powerless and I'm so sick of feeling that way, so I'm going to say the worst thing possible so you can feel how I feel!"

That sounds about right, doesn't it? You may not be the type of person who says these things out loud, but even if you're thinking them, the thoughts come from feelings of fear and powerlessness.

> When we insult people, we're actually losing, rather than gaining, control.

Think about a time when you were rude or insulting to one of your parents. Use your journal or the blank pages at the end of the book to write down your thoughts.

Describe what happened. Who said what?

What was the first wrong move you made?

How could you handle it differently if it happens again?

Notice that I'm not saying it was your fault.

I'm not saying your parent(s) didn't also have a part in the situation. I'm just asking you to look at your part.

(This is pretty advanced stuff. There are many adults who don't know how to do this either. So if this is kinda confusing, that's okay. Try discussing it with a friend.)

OPINIONS VS. BEING RIGHT

Opinions are harmless in and of themselves; they're just judgments we have about a situation, place, idea, or person.

We get into trouble when we try to impose our opinion on someone else, thinking it's a fact.

It isn't.

If it were a fact, it would be called a fact, not an opinion.

Even if someone asks for your opinion, it doesn't mean they're asking you to prove how wrong they are.

There's an old saying, "You catch more flies with honey than with vinegar." This means if you want someone to see things your way or to do something for you or with you, it's more effective to be sweet than to be a jerk or a know-it-all.

What about when someone tries to impose his or her opinion on you?

Needing to be right, pushing our opinion on someone else – these are signs of insecurity and, yes, Fear. And it's just plain rude. There are ways to share our opinions that are less aggressive. For instance, we can join a group that does community work supporting a cause we believe in. Or we can donate to a charity, political, or religious group with whom we agree. Or we can vote.

Similarly, we can choose (with practice) to not be dragged into a "festival" of insults. Writer Miguel Ruiz asserts:

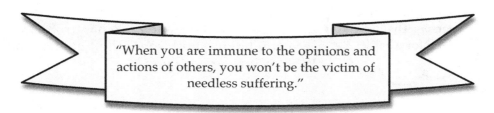

"When you are immune to the opinions and actions of others, you won't be the victim of needless suffering."

Instead, when someone tries to change your opinion, you can say, "Everyone is entitled to their opinion." Or, "Thank you." And leave it at that. No matter how ridiculous the other person's thinking is, there will only be trouble when we expect the other person to change their mind.

I am reminded of the time when a playful conversation between sisters (Harry Potter vs. Twilight) turned dramatic and ended with insults and with one sister in tears.

Such a waste of time and energy. You just never know the outcome of pushing your opinion on someone else.

Think about a time when you were pretty forceful about your opinion. Do some writing on it.

Describe what happened. Who said what?

What was the first wrong move you made?

How could you handle it differently if it happens again?

QUESTIONS VS. DEMANDS

I know you know this one.
A question is a request for information. Where teens and parents get into trouble is when they use the form of a question to challenge each other or to make a demand.

Demands challenge the other person. That's a set-up for a battle.

Instead of parents asking, "What's upsetting you?" they demand, "Stop talking to me that way!" Instead of asking, "What problems are you having with school?" they demand, "What is wrong with you?"

And what about teens?

Instead of asking, "When will I be old enough to get a cell phone?" you demand, "Why can't I have a cell phone?"

Instead of asking if or when it would be okay for you to have a later curfew, you demand, "How come Robby gets a later curfew, but not me?"

You could be calm and respectful but instead you choose to be irritating and unpleasant.

Why do you do that??

Life could be so much easier.

And how many times do you make demands when you know the answer?

Demands are LOUD questions. Demands are MEAN questions. Demands are REPEATED questions.

It's not like you were just dropped into the family. You've probably lived there for a while. You know what your parents will probably say in response to your demands.

It is a huge waste of time, energy, and good feelings demanding things *(or repeatedly asking for things)* that you know you're never going to get.

"No, you can't date when you're 12!"

"No, you can't get a tattoo or piercing before you're 16!"

"No, we're not buying you a motorcycle!"

Why fight it?

Even if you get your way, you've done it at your own expense. You've just taken on the role of "pain in the neck."

Is that really how you want to be seen?

Wouldn't you rather be seen as "cool and wonderful daughter (or son) with whom I love to hang out?"

You know you wouldn't act this way with a friend or probably even a grandparent. Why do you do it with your parents?

Think of a recent experience when you demanded something instead of asking a question about it:

Describe what happened. Who said what?

What was the first wrong move you made?

How could you handle it differently if it happens again?

HONESTY VS. LYING

Why did I include this one? It seems pretty logical that telling the truth is good and lying is bad, right?

Wrong.
If it were that simple, people wouldn't lie, deny, omit, and blame others with   such frequency.

> Lying is often about self-protection, not "other-rejection."

Lying is, actually, complicated and it drives both parents and teens up a wall. You all go absolutely ballistic when lied to. B.A.L.L.I.S.T.I.C.
You take it personally when it's not really about you. You are horrified and repulsed by the liar.

Except when you do it yourself. Then there's a good reason for doing it (wink, wink).

After watching teens and parents lie for quite a few years now and I've come to some conclusions (feel free to share this with your parents):

Parents and teens lie because:

✓ They're afraid of the truth.
✓ They're ashamed of themselves or feel they're not good enough.
✓ They think they're protecting the other person.
✓ They're afraid the other person will hate them when they find out the truth.

✓ Putting off revealing the truth means putting off having to face reality.

✓ They're hoping that by the time the other person finds out, things will have improved.

Sure, sometimes people lie because they're "evil" or immoral. It does happen. But notice that the reasons I've listed above are not about disrespecting the other person but, rather, disrespecting oneself. It's harder and harder to feel okay being you.

When I'm working with teens and their parents, I like to look at lying as a self-esteem issue rather than a moral issue.

As I've said, both parents and teens can be dishonest, and for the same reasons, but they simply hate dishonesty in the other.

When it comes to teens, lying is more of a self-esteem issue, than a moral issue.

You've got parents withholding information who are screaming at their kids for doing the same thing. And you've got teens who are appalled and disgusted by hypocrisy, when they're omitting important facts from their conversations with their parents.

Marcus was always a good student but he had a secret that took up his time and thoughts. He couldn't concentrate on his schoolwork.

Instead, he treated his parents like it was their fault that his grades were dropping. He told them that he didn't want to be on ADHD medication anymore and that they shouldn't bug him about schoolwork.

Since that wasn't the truth, that didn't work. It's not what he really needed. One day, Marcus broke down at school and called his mom to pick him up. On the ride home, he told her his secret – that he was gay.

His parents had known this for some time but were trying to respect Marcus's privacy. In a way, they were lying too, by not telling him that they knew.

Once they were all telling the truth, they could stop focusing on schoolwork (which was a comparatively minor issue) and could focus on recreating the family harmony they once had.

Even the nicest kids lie sometimes. Telling the truth is scary.

Here are some thoughts that should make it easier:

- ✓ Telling the truth can be a big relief. Keeping secrets is exhausting.
- ✓ Telling the truth gets you into less trouble than lying.
- ✓ Lies are hard to keep track of.
- ✓ Once you start lying, it's hard to stop.
- ✓ Lots of times people are more upset that you *lied* about what you did than they are about the actual thing that you did.

Some conversations are painful to have, but it's important to remember that your parents love you very much. Its impossible for me to express in words just how much they love you. Truly, it's an immeasurable amount.

For most of you, if you had a big problem, your parents would drop everything to help. What I find, though, is that often teens will say, "I'm fine. Everything's fine. Nothing's wrong." When actually, help is just what you yearn for.

Lying and hiding keep us feeling terrible about ourselves and the world. Instead, we could be spending our time feeling strong and capable and happy.

What about those times when someone asks for the truth but it would probably hurt his or her feelings? *Remember this: honesty without kindness is cruelty. Be as kind as possible.*

Think of a time you lied, when telling the truth would have been so much better.

Describe what happened. How were you feeling?

What made you think you should lie?

How could you handle it differently if it happens again?

If you feel you can't tell your parents the truth, for whatever reason, find a trustworthy adult to talk to: a teacher, coach, school counselor, or therapist. It is not uncommon for school counselors or coaches to be the first to hear about a pregnancy scare, a party that got out of control, or even a bad grade. These adults can help you talk to your parents, without taking sides, and can offer support for you and encouragement for your parents.

If, in an extreme example, your parent has done something illegal or immoral, these adults can protect your identity and arrange for some sort of intervention for your family.

HEARING VS. LISTENING

Hearing is done with your ears. It's a physiological function. Listening is done with your ears, your mind, and your heart. It is physiological, mental, and emotional.

Your parents can deliver the same piece of information to you and, depending on whether you're hearing or listening, you can have an easy moment or a tense moment.

> Real listening is fearless.

For example, your father says, "Hey, I'm really sorry. I had a longer day than I thought I would and I didn't get to the store on time to pick up your thingamabob."

If you're just hearing what he says, you will focus on the part about him not getting you what you wanted, because that's the part of his sentence that revolves around you. You might respond with an insult or a demand.

If you're listening, however, you can hear everything he said, including:

- ✓ How he had an extra-long day (he must be so tired)
- ✓ He's feeling bad that he couldn't do what he said he would do (he said he was sorry), and
- ✓ How much he loves you (he didn't forget the thingamabob; he just couldn't get it).

Real listening is:

- ✓ **Attentive:** You need to actually pay attention. You can nod your head and say little things like "Hmmmm" or "Wow!" or "Yeah? Really?" or "Phew!" You want to be careful not to interrupt, of course.

- ✓ **Non-judgmental:** You don't have to agree with them, but don't judge them as being wrong or stupid or bad.

- ✓ **Non-correcting:** Teens and parents can spend a lot of time trying to convince the other person of their point of view. It's not helpful and prolongs the misery of miscommunication. Don't correct them; just listen. *This also means you don't have to solve your parents' problems, because really, that's their job.*

- ✓ **Loving, rather than defensive:** Assume the best. If it sounds like an attack, assume it's fear speaking. You may feel the urge to run or to stay and fight, but try to stay and connect with your own heart. Use your breathing to calm yourself down, and your mirror neurons to calm down the whole situation.

- ✓ **Self-reflective:** Conversations and heart-to-heart communications give you the chance to grow and learn more about yourself. Take these opportunities to ask yourself, "What's my part?" and "Can I be doing something differently, or have I been the best ME I can be?"

Real listening is fearless listening. Fear tells us to attack, judge, yell, deny, lecture, or interrupt. Fearless listening means hearing and accepting what's being shared. It requires vulnerability and that can be scary.

Think of a time when you heard what was said but you didn't really listen:

Describe what happened. Who said what?

What did you hear?

What was the speaker really trying to say?

How could you handle it differently if it happens again?

CONVERSATIONS VS. POWER STRUGGLES

We often think that having a conversation should be easy. First you open your mouth and say something, then the other person opens their mouth and says something. And so on, and so on. Simple.

But conversing involves much more than flapping our gums. It involves understanding and appreciation. If you are misunderstood, if your message is offensive rather than interesting or inspiring, people won't listen.

What frequently happens between teens and parents is that arguing and power struggles replace true conversation. It's hard to feel safe enough to have a conversation when you think you're going to be attacked. That's one reason there is so much miscommunication; you're preparing to attack or be attacked. It's hard to get your point across that way.

A conversation is a calm talk about thoughts, feelings, opinion, likes, dislikes, plans, and goals.

A conversation is *not* a time to:

✓ Give advice (unless asked)

✓ Insult or hurt people

✓ Interrupt

✓ Explain your viewpoint over and over again

✓ Yell, whine, scold, complain, demand, attack, or argue

Conversations are not about trying to control another person.

These are all examples of trying to control another person. If you're trying to control another person, or they're trying to control you, it's not a conversation; it's a power struggle.

(For translation's sake, when you are disrespectful or you talk on and on and on, or you say "NO!" parents consider that yelling. Just like you consider nagging and lecturing to be yelling).

**There are two kinds of parent-teen conversations:
Teen-initiated and parent-initiated.**

PREPARING FOR TEEN-INITIATED CONVERSATIONS

These are conversations that you begin. Even though we're practicing how to talk to your parents, these tips will work for any conversation, like:

✓ Getting information from a professor or employer

✓ Making new friends

✓ Having difficult conversations with current friends

✓ Asking someone out on a date

✓ Talking to your favorite celebrity

Starting a conversation with your parents can be a bit nerve-jangling, but it's important to realize that, when your parents have to start a conversation with you, they're nervous as well. They so want you to be happy and healthy and successful, and they worry that if they say the wrong thing they'll ruin your chance to have a good life. "Starting a Conversation With Your Teen" is a topic I deal with a lot when I'm working with parents, and I do the same thing that I'm doing here with you. I walk them through it.

These tips will help you start a conversation with just about anyone.

So if you're worried, it's okay. Part of maturing into a healthy person is facing (or even embracing) your challenges.

HOW DO YOU START A CONVERSATION?

Some people get the ball rolling by leaving a note saying something like, "I'd like to talk to you when you get a chance," or "Can we talk about X (some topic) later today?"

Others just go up to the person and say, "I'd like to talk to you" or "When's a good time to talk to you?" Stating the topic is good too.

When you're actually sitting down to talk, you might say, "I was just thinking about this and wondered what your thoughts are," or simply, "I was wondering . . . "

In addition to the tips from Day Five (belly-breathing, talking to your fear, etc.), here are some practical skills to turn you into an expert conversationalist:

Think in terms of "intention" rather than "agenda."

An agenda is a plan or a map.

It takes you from the beginning of something to the end.

For instance, your teacher may write the class agenda on the board each day. But when there's an agenda, there's a leader, and conversations don't have leaders.

Remember, if you go into a conversation with a demand or with the goal of changing someone's thinking or personality, it stops being a conversation.

At the same time, it's good to know why you're having the conversation.

> Your intention is what you bring to the conversation.

Your intention is more like what you hope to bring to the conversation. How many times do you start talking to your parents and then something happens and it all falls apart? You thought you were all having fun, but you end up grounded!

Going into a conversation with an intention will help you be more conscious of what you're saying so you don't get off track.

Conversations are about creating some sort of connection. Set your intention to create the bond, or to get closer to your parents, or to express your thoughts without any expectations and you'll be better off.

In fact, you can't really set an intention to get what you want because now there's someone else involved. It would be like saying, "I intend for my teacher to get a cold." That's not in your power!

You can't change another person, but when you set an intention to communicate better, that means *you're setting the intention to be a better communicator, and you can change yourself.* This is a win-win!

Watch your body language and tone of voice.

We tend to think of language as just what comes out of our mouths, but how many times do your parents get mad at you for something, and you say, "But I didn't say anything!" And they might reply, "But you were thinking it!"

They're noticing something you didn't intend for them to notice! That's because we speak with more than our mouths.

Here are things teens and parents do with their bodies that can easily bug:

- ✓ Rolling your eyes
- ✓ Shaking your head
- ✓ Standing with your hands on your hips
- ✓ Leaning towards a person when you're angry at them
- ✓ Leaning back when you don't want to hear what's being said
- ✓ Sitting slumped down with your arms crossed.
- ✓ Making noises with your mouth that sound like you're disgusted (sighing loudly, for example)

Check your body language and tone of voice by recording yourself and listening to or watching the playback.

How about tone of voice?

Some people know when their tone is mean or challenging or bored to death; some people don't. If people often say that you can't hear yourself or that your tone is rude, try recording yourself.

Here's what to listen for:

- ✓ Sarcasm or trying to be funny in a slightly nasty way.
- ✓ Using a "know-it-all voice" or sounding like what you just heard was really dumb or obvious.
- ✓ Whining, or
- ✓ Speaking in a level, calm, or monotone voice while saying condescending or insulting things.

Keep the language light and polite.

Both you and your parent might be a bit nervous. That's natural. But when you throw in a bunch of slang or swear words (or if *they* do) it alienates the listener, and you lose the thread of the conversation. Now everyone's focused on your weird word choices and not on your message and your intention.

You can make this easier by leaving out language that makes your parents uncomfortable or makes you look like just another mouthy teenager.

Sometimes parents and teens speak in a very calm, rational-sounding voice *but the content of their message is very rude.* Rude is rude, even if you say it with the most polite-sounding voice in the world.

> Rude is Rude, even if you sound like a king, queen, judge, or minister when you're talking.

For example, I've heard teens say, "With all due respect" or "Not to be insulting" and then they come out with something completely disrespectful and insulting! You can't say, "With all due respect, your idea is stupid" and expect to be taken seriously. Just saying nice words doesn't mean you're being nice.

I've also heard a parent calmly explain to her teen, "If you continue this way you'll just end up a stupid b*tch." And then the mom said to me, "I was calm. I wasn't yelling. I didn't call her a b*tch. I said if she continued her behavior, she'd *become* a b*tch. There's a difference."

Uh, no. No difference.
People, people, people: Light and polite, please.

Not all conversations have to be heavy-duty. It's okay (and very impressive) to just ask your parents, "How was work today?" or "Did you and your friend do anything fun?" or "How 'bout those 'Hawks / Yankees / Angels / Vikings / (other sports team)?"

Timing is crucial.

We talked about timing in Day Five. Parents don't like to be ambushed any more than you do. Don't try to converse with your parents when they're angry, stressed, super focused or super busy. That is bad timing. They won't be able to concentrate and the conversation is likely to turn out badly.

One technique is to ask them, "Is this a good time to talk?" or you can sort of make an appointment to talk. Then you have a greater chance of getting their full attention and their good will, and they'll be awed and pretty darn delighted by your maturity!

Clarity.

Knowing what you're going to say ahead of time will help you get your message across the way you want to. It's a great technique to practice in front of a mirror. If you have privacy, you'll feel more comfortable practicing over and over again. In fact, most public speakers do just that. They rehearse a lot.

"Expectations are planned disappointments."

Remember that if you go into a conversation expecting a certain result, acting over-confident and showing your swagger, or assuming that you know exactly how to get your parents to do what you want, then you are trying to control the situation and control your parents.

Of course the same goes for parents.

Don't you hate when they swagger in and say, "You'll do it because I said so!" Or when they make some random new rule and expect you to be excited about it.

You know how it feels. Why do it?

THE CONVERSATION TOPICS

The next step is to actually start having conversations with your parents. Communicating well means having more than one conversation and calling it done!

Training your parents, much like training anything else, including dogs, plants, or your hair, takes ongoing effort.

> Having a good conversation is a skill. You can't train your dog once and be done. Neither can you have one good conversation with your parents and think everything is fixed.

Try starting with a bunch of short but sweet, light and polite talks ("Hi Dad, how was your day?" "Hi Mom, did you do anything fun today?") and then you'll be ready for longer discussions.

Much as I did for Day Five, I've divided the conversation topics by parent type, but these topics are more varied. (Also, in the back of the book, I've added 101 extra conversation topics so you can continue your training!)

For each type of parent, there are three topics to get you started and then two more "advanced" topics.

Many parents like it when their kids ask to hear stories about the parent's childhood or ask their opinion about something. Many don't. Some parents are uncomfortable when asked about their feelings. Some are not.

This is why I suggest you start with one or two of the "getting started" topics and then work your way up to the "advanced" ones.

It's okay if it takes you several days to get through all the questions. It may even take weeks or months, and that's okay too.

Watch how your parents react to the questions. This will show you their comfort level and then you can set the pace based on that.

Your parent's comfort level is, in fact, more important than your own here. Training your parents means really seeing them as everyday human beings.

115

Taking their feelings into consideration is something that kids don't always do (even adult kids). No one likes to be pushed or controlled, so don't try to push or control your parents, even if you're just really eager to get through all the exercises as soon as possible.

If your parents seem uncomfortable, slow down.

Remember: use your parents' comfort level as a cue. You don't want to go too fast.

Communicating with Disciplinarian Parents

On the one hand, these parents can be more formal and more self-protective. On the other hand, they may be overbearing and smothering. They may love you deeply, but they're often thinking about "the rules" and whether everyone is following them. Disclosing a lot of personal information may be very difficult for them. Having a conversation with you instead of lecturing you may be challenging. Be patient and don't push.

Getting Started:

What do you like best about your job?

What do you like doing more than anything else?

What is your dream vacation?

Advanced:

What do you like best about yourself?

What's the best decision you ever made?

Communicating with Distracted Parents

Distracted parents can focus on things that excite them, so their questions are about things that might get them thinking in a fun way.

Keep the questions a mix of open-ended and specific, like "I'd like to spend more time talking to you about what's important to you. Like, what do you love the most about your life?"

That way, your parent can choose to talk about what he or she thinks is important, or just answer your questions.

Getting Started:

What is the most exciting thing in your life?

What do you love the most about your life?

If you could go anywhere in the world where would you go?

Advanced:

What's your dream career?

Is there anything you don't like about yourself?

Communicating with Permissive Parents

When the timing is right, you can go pretty deep with permissive parents because, generally, they want a close connection with their kids.

Getting Started:

What were your parents like?

What's one thing you would change about your parents?

If you could take a dream family vacation, what would we do?

Advanced:

What do you like the most about being a parent?

What scares you the most about being a parent?

Communicating with Even-Handed Parents

You will probably get some really honest and thoughtful answers to your questions. Typically, even-handed parents aren't afraid to share their thoughts with their kids.

As I mentioned on Day Two, some topics are private, but while other parents might shut down or get angry or fidgety when you ask a highly personal question, even-handed parents will just let you know they don't want to answer that particular question.

Getting Started:

What are a few of your proudest accomplishments?

What's the easiest part about being a parent?

What's the hardest part about being a parent?

Advanced:

Did your parents do anything that made you say: "I want to be just like them"?

Did they do anything that made you say, "I don't ever want to do that"?

Communicating with Disconnected Parents

Remember that disconnected parents aren't always disconnected, but you need to tread lightly and accept the fact that they won't always be available to talk with you.

Start with one question and make it an easy one, like a YES or NO question, or a question with a one-word answer. If they want to add anything, they will.

Be kind of casual, like you're okay if they don't answer. Disconnected parents don't do well with pressure.

By the way, if any of their answers don't mention you, try not to take it personally.

Getting Started:

When you were younger, did you like school/sports/your siblings?

If you could meet a famous person, who would it be?

What's the coolest thing you've ever done?

Advanced:

If you won the lottery, what would you do with the money?

What would a perfect day look like for you?

PREPARING FOR PARENT-INITIATED CONVERSATIONS

Unfortunately, you can't always control when and how your parents start conversations! They may bring up something in front of your siblings. They may bring up something in front of your friends.

The good news is you can prepare by keeping these tips in mind:

✓ **If you know your parents tend to be random about choosing times to talk**, politely let them know (after the conversation, not during, because interrupting is rude) that you would really appreciate some notice so when they talk to you, you can give them your full attention and not be distracted. (Get it? You're telling them you want to listen to them.)

✓ **Stay calm and polite**. Conversations go faster and are less painful when you're calm and polite. You'll feel better about yourself *and them*, surprisingly.

✓ **If your parents are asking you a lot of questions** about your day, it means they're interested in you. Parents aren't always trying to spy on you. Enjoy it. If you had a parent that neglected you or only talked about him/herself, you wouldn't be happy.

Parents ask questions to bond with you. They don't want to lose the closeness you once had just because you're older. *If you answer their questions, they'll actually ask fewer, not more!*

✓ **If you don't like being asked a bunch of questions**, the *perfect solution* is to volunteer the information in the first place!

When you come home or they come home, take some time to talk about your day. Tell them some interesting things you learned or some funny things that happened. They'll stop asking if you start telling. *Guaranteed!*

✓ **Want to stop the nagging?** If you do your homework, chores, etc. before you're asked, they won't have to nag you.

Parents tend to get pretty bent out of shape when you ignore your commitments and responsibilities.

You know that.
So, stop it.

Stop choosing to get nagged, and start choosing to get more rewards.
There can be more than one good kid in a family.

✓ *Even if your parents end up disagreeing with you or saying no to a request, you've still succeeded.* The idea is to get your parents to take you seriously. That comes first.

After they're used to taking you seriously, they'll be inclined to trust you more. If you continue to whine and complain, you won't get the freedom you crave.

No-nos for parent-initiated conversations

✓ **You're busy** with homework or chores, or you have a friend over and your parents want to talk to you. Don't whine and say, "I'm busy. I can't talk now." Instead, ask if you can talk to them in 10 or 15 minutes. Don't put them off too long; they're your parents after all.

✓ **Your parents remind you** to do your chores or get started with your homework, or stop bullying your brother or sister. Don't get huffy and act insulted. You know the rules in your house.

✓ **You've decided** that you don't feel like doing your chores or your homework so you try to find a loophole like "It's a school holiday" or "It's snowing" or "I start a new school next week so homework at this school doesn't matter" or "Brother/Sister didn't do his/her chores and you didn't say anything!"

You know you have chores. You're making yourself look bad.

✓ **Your parents come up with a great idea** like no TV on Sundays or something like that. Maybe it's a good idea, maybe it's not, but you start objecting to it right away.

You call it "explaining," but you're really arguing and trying to get them to change their minds. Basically what you've done is tell them you think they're stupid and that you're much more clever so they should listen to you.

Really?

Now what parent is going to listen to you after that?
You've disrespected them but now they're supposed to respect you? Hmmm.

Do you see how much control you have?

You can *choose* your response.
If you choose to whine or complain (which is a teen version of nagging, by the way), don't get mad at *them!*

Just choose differently next time.

You don't have to argue.
You have choices.
And if you want to start training your parents then you'll have to start making some good ones.

Sooner, rather than later, I hope. ☺

WHAT IF, AFTER ALL THIS GUIDANCE, YOU STILL FEEL LIKE YOU'RE NOT READY?

You may be afraid or your gut may be telling you this is not a good time to start a conversation.
It's okay.

If training your parents takes a bit longer *(or a lot longer)* that's okay. **Just reading the book and doing the exercises can improve your relationship with your parents.**

And if you get to the point where you want more, you can always go deeper, do a little more.

There's only one way to do this wrong and that's if you jump ahead and do the later exercises before the early ones. (And, frankly, "wrong" is probably not a good word. I mean, it's not like your head will explode or someone will die.)

The deal is, unless you give your parents this book to read, and unless they read it, you're the one who's going to be training them, which means *you need to be the change, not the problem.*

Follow your heart, go at your own pace, breathe in some courage from all the people who adore you, and take the next step, whatever that may be for you.

THINKING ABOUT DAY SIX

Phew.

You learned tons and tons today, didn't you? Who, what, when, where, why, and how to communicate with your parents.

What was the most helpful thing you learned today?

Was there something you've known, but never really admitted? (Like about lying? That would have been mine at your age.)

Which part was the most fun (or the *least not-fun*)?

What ideas do you think you'll share with your friends?

What did you learn about your parents that you want to remember, and that you might even want to tell your own kids someday?

NOW WHAT?

> "If I tell my father I love him, then he wins." Lee, age 35
>
> "All my mother talks about is tennis and food. Tennis and food. She never asks about my interests." Sandy, age 49

You read these quotes right?

You see these people are both adults, right?

How would you like to be in your 30s or 40s and still be complaining about your parents?

I can make that happen, if you're interested. Just do the opposite of everything in this book!

What you see in these two people is FEAR.

They're afraid that if they let go of their anger and resentment, their parents will gain enormous amounts of power and they (the adult kids) will be crushed.

They're creating their own limitations by assuming that their fears are fact.

These folks have never chosen to turn their childhood relationships with their parents into something more mature, more sustainable, and much more enjoyable.

How amazing for you to choose to change your relationships while you're still relatively young. How empowering to simply bypass any adult heartache you might have had.

You now have a whole bag of tricks and strategies and scripts to help you understand, communicate, and connect with your parents.

You know what makes them tick, what they fear, where you miscommunicate, and how to fix your miscommunications with clear, honest and kind-hearted conversation.

The poet, E. E. Cummings wrote:

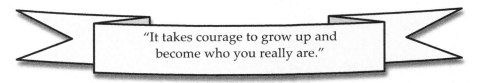

"It takes courage to grow up and
become who you really are."

With that in mind, here are two lessons I'd like to leave you with:

1. **Surround yourself with people who love you no matter what.** They smile or light up when they see you. They ask how you're doing and are excited about your successes. You don't have to do anything except be your true, authentic, *imperfect* self.

    They even love you if you have nothing to offer. They don't need your money, your property, your fame, your intellect, your skills, your body, or your soul. That is truly Love.

2. **Ask for help.** It's okay. We live in communities and communities look out for one another. If you take the time, you will always find people who want to help you. They may not look like what you think they should look like. They may not look like what you want them to look like. But you'll find they will be ready, willing, and able to give you a hand, support your interests, offer good counsel, and encourage your efforts.

You have so many choices now – you've got all the power you need to create an amazing relationship with just about anyone.

You don't need to try to force your power on anyone or try to steal more from someone else. It's yours. You are strong and wonderful and capable of love and joy and FUN!

Now go forth and be awesome!

Your fan,

Margit Crane

Seattle, 2011

MORE GOODIES

MORE FUN:
101 CONVERSATION STARTERS*
Family fun when you're just hanging out

1. What is your earliest memory?
2. What do you like best about your job/school?
3. What's the best decision you've made, so far?
4. If you could go anywhere in the world, where would you go?
5. If you could take a dream family vacation, what would we do?
6. If you had to spend a million dollars in two days, how would you spend it?
7. If you could choose another name (first or last), what would it be?
8. If you chose a nickname for yourself, what would it be?
9. If you could change anything about yourself, what would it be?
10. What are you afraid of?
11. Who are a few people you admire?
12. What are your 3 all-time favorite books?
13. Who are your 3 all-time favorite bands or singers?
14. What are your 3 all-time favorite TV shows?
15. What are your 3 all-time favorite movies?
16. If your life had a theme song, which song what you choose?
17. If your life were a movie, which actor/actress would you want to play you?
18. Which actor would you want to play your father?
19. Which actress would play your mother?
20. If you have stepparents, who would play them?
21. What would you like to be famous for?
22. What would you like to do better?
23. What makes you angry?
24. What's your favorite smell or scent?
25. What's your least favorite smell or scent?
26. What job would you least like to do?
27. What job would you most like to do? (If you love your job, what other job would you want to try?)
28. What color best represents your personality?
29. What are your 5 favorite foods?
30. What are your 5 least favorite foods?
31. What food have you not tasted, but you would like to try?
32. What's your favorite drink?
33. What food could you eat every day?
34. What's the most disgusting thing you've ever eaten?
35. What is a favorite food you could live without?
36. If you were dying, what would you want for your last meal?

37. What country in the world best represents your personality?
38. What sound do you love?
39. What sound do you hate?
40. What cartoon character are you?
41. Which character in a movie would you like to be?
42. Where is your favorite place to be?
43. Where is your least favorite place to be?
44. What do you wish your mom would say to you that she hasn't said yet?
45. What do you wish your dad would say to you that he hasn't said yet?
46. What is something about you that most people don't know?
47. What type of music best represents your personality?
48. What type or genre of literature best represents your personality?
49. Choose an animal whose qualities you wish you had.
50. What's your favorite word?
51. What's your least favorite word?
52. Who is your favorite actor?
53. Who is your favorite actress?
54. What movie title best represents your personality or your life?
55. What book title best represents your personality or your life?
56. What do you want written on your tombstone?
57. What 3 things (other than technology) would you take out of your house if it were burning down?
58. What's a piece of technology you *could* live without?
59. What do you think is the secret to success?
60. Which relative (not immediate family) are you closest to?
61. What would your best friend say is your best quality?
62. What would your best friend say is your worst quality?
63. What is the best compliment that anyone can pay you?
64. What compliment, while nice, really doesn't mean much to you?
65. If someone wanted to insult you, what would hurt the most?
66. If someone tried to insult you, what wouldn't hurt at all?
67. What is the nicest thing you did for someone in the past week?
68. What is the nicest thing you've ever done for someone?
69. What's the nicest thing someone did for you this week?
70. What's the nicest thing someone ever did for you? (Aside from giving birth to you!)
71. Mountain, beach, forest, desert, countryside - which do you prefer?
72. Would you rather live on a boat, in a tent, in a condo, or in a house?
73. If you could create a charity organization, what would the Cause be?

74. If you could meet a famous living person, who would it be?
75. What would you ask him or her?
76. If you could meet a famous dead person, who would it be?
77. What would you ask him or her?
78. What's your favorite season?
79. If you could live in another city, state, or country, which would you choose?
80. If you could live in another era – past or future – which would you choose?
81. What WOW moment did you have this week?
82. If you had the skill to play any sport, which would you choose?
83. What's your favorite board or card game?
84. If you had to give up one of your senses, which would it be?
85. Which of your personality traits gets you into the most trouble?
86. What makes you laugh the most?
87. What is your favorite hot-weather activity?
88. What is your favorite cold-weather activity?
89. What is your favorite quote?
90. What was your most embarrassing moment? (I know, tricky)
91. What invention would make your life easier?
92. What's your best friend's best quality?
93. Describe a recurring dream you have.
94. When you first meet someone, what are you most afraid they'll think about your appearance, or your personality, or whatever?
95. If you had 1 day left to live, what would you do that day?
96. What do you/did you like best about going back to school after the summer?
97. What pleasantly surprised you the most this week or this month?
98. If you could have any animal as a pet, which would you choose?
99. Painting, photography, sculpture, drawing, graphic design – which would you rather be great at?
100. Dancing, singing, acting - which would you rather be great at?
101. What 3 things are you grateful for?

* Don't forget to explain your answers!

MORE FANS:

IS ANYBODY LISTENING?
5 TIPS FOR FINDING TRUSTWORTHY ADULTS
Find a good team of adults to support & encourage you

DO ANY OF THESE SOUND FAMILIAR?

> "Life is so big and I don't really get where I fit in."
>
> "Sure, things are great now, but what happens when I'm on my own?"
>
> "I want to be successful but I'm not really sure where to start."
>
> "Some stuff is private; I would be embarrassed to talk to my parents about it."
>
> I have so many questions! If only I had someone to talk to who could really listen."

Of course you want someone to talk to; we all do, if we're perfectly honest with ourselves. Sure, you can talk to your friends but when you really need help, especially about "adult topics," your friends will listen and they'll sympathize, but will they have solutions?

Solutions are pretty hard to get from someone who hasn't solved any of these issues for themselves yet.

To make it through all the very real teenage angst, it's important to talk to someone who has been through it all before you – someone successful. I don't mean money-successful or popularity-successful (although those are good too). I'm talking about someone who is happy with his/her life, someone who feels whole and content. *And, frankly, chances are good that that's an adult.*

You're not always going to live at home. The trick, then, is to find adults you can trust, who will give you careful and caring guidance, but won't try to control you or change you.

They may be teachers, professors, counselors, coaches, clergy, employers, or co-workers. Their title isn't as important as their character.

Check out these 5 tips for finding trustworthy adults, and build your "mentor-seeking skills."

1. Watch how they are with others, either people your age or their own friends. Adults who are mean or who make fun of people may be entertaining to observe but they aren't trustworthy. Anyone who needs to belittle others, even if they tell you they "have a good reason," is much more interested in their own needs than they could ever be in yours.

2. Adults should keep their hands to themselves. A pat on the back is cool, but a hand on your leg? Ewww. Hugging is okay, if you know them already, but adults shouldn't hang all over teens! The tricky thing here is that it feels good when an adult you like pays attention to you. It may seem like they're just being extra nice, but remember: they're adults and they know what's inappropriate. To ignore that and just do whatever they feel like means they're putting their own needs above yours. Not only are they using you, they are ABusing you (and they know it).

3. Are they friendly with a variety of people, or just young people? A healthy adult can get along with many different kinds of people. That's pretty much part of the definition of an adult! (Notice that I'm talking about emotional age, not chronological age here.) Real adults are able to enjoy relationships with other adults; they can successfully begin, sustain, and even end meaningful relationships without damaging themselves or others.

4. Do they try to get you to do anything you don't want to do? I'm not just talking about trying to get you to do sexual stuff. What I mean is, are they really bossing you around, or are they just trying to get you to do your part? It makes sense for a parent, relative, guardian or family friend to ask you to chip in on the chores and do your part. Even taking out the trash or cleaning the bathroom is logical. Someone's got to do it!

   But if cruelty – that is, repeated insults, mockery, or physical intimidation – is commonplace in your relationships, those adults cannot be trusted with your deepest feelings. They may deserve your love; you may need to show them respect. But they are not behaving in a trustworthy manner.

5. If an adult offers you drugs or alcohol or porn they are not interested in helping you. In fact, they're not interested in you AT ALL. Even if they are parents of your best friends or they are your own parents' best friends, they are not to be trusted. I don't care how cool they may seem, no matter how much it seems like you're being respected as an equal, there is not a trustworthy adult on the planet who would offer a teenager something so obviously inappropriate.

What's next?

Well, if you're lucky, you may find you have trustworthy adults right in your family, or your parents may have a friend or two you can trust. If not, you can use this checklist and your gut or intuition to start "interviewing" adults.

It's not like a real interview, but you're going to want to ask some questions and see how they answer them so you can find out something about their lives and their personalities.

You don't have to get into any deep topics or reveal any of your private life. If you just keep talking and listening you will have a "gut feeling" when something feels off or odd. It may be a rush of adrenalin or a queasy stomach or a voice in your head telling you to be cautious. *Trust that.*

If you feel you can't wait to interview a bunch of adults, there are adults in your school who will help you if you are scared or in pain. They may not be the coolest or the most interesting. They may dress funny or have a comb-over, or wear too much make-up, or have bad breath. But if you need them, they are there, ready to give you the kindness and direction you need, without asking for anything in return.

MORE HELP:
HOTLINE AND HELPLINE NUMBERS
If you need help, these people want to help you

Adolescent Crisis Intervention & Counseling
"The Nine-Line"
1-800-999-9999 (it's a real number)

Al-Anon/Alateen Hotline
Hope and Help for young people who are the relatives & friends of a problem drinker
1-800-344-2666

Alcohol/Drug Abuse Hotline
1-800-662-HELP (-4357)

Boys Town National Hotline
For troubled kids & families
1-800-448-3000

Child Abuse Hotline
1-800-4-A-CHILD
(1-800-422-4453)

Domestic Violence Hotline
1-800-799-SAFE (-7233)

Emergency Contraception Info
1-888-NOT-2-LATE
(1-888-668-2528)

Gay, Lesbian, Bisexual and Transgender (GLBT) Youth Support Line
1-800-850-8078

Help Finding a Therapist
1-800-THERAPIST
(1-800-843-7274)

National Adolescent Suicide Hotline
1-800-621-4000

Nat'l Eating Disorders Helpline
1-800-931-2237

National Runaway Switchboard & Suicide Hotline
1-800-621-4000

Nat'l Teen Dating Abuse Help
LoveIsRespect.org
(virtual helpline)
1-866-331-9474

MORE RESOURCES:
BOOKS & WEBSITES I LOVE!
(I think you'll like them too.)

TeenAdvice.com
Info on subjects that interest teens!

SelfCounseling.com
More info on subjects that interest teens!

Thomas Armstrong
7 Kinds of Smart: Identifying and Developing Your Many Intelligences.
There are many ways to be smart, not just book-smart or school-smart. Learn which intelligences you excel in and how to strengthen them.

Kathryn D. Cramer, PhD and Hank Wasiak
Change the Way You See Everything, for Teens
A fun and interesting book with exercises to explore how you see the world, from the Asset-Based Thinking® Cramer Institute.

Susan Gregg
The Complete Idiot's Guide to Short Meditations
I love these meditations and visualizations because they're short and effective.

Thích Nhât Hanh
Anger: Wisdom for Cooling the Flames
I used this book in my Anger Management support groups and the teens loved the author's simple but deep wisdom.

Tom Rath
StrengthsFinder 2.0
I use this book with most of my teen clients and their parents. It has an online questionnaire about your preferences. It then gives you your top 5 strengths or life themes. I've never met anyone who wasn't thoroughly pleased with the results. (My #1 Life-Theme? *Communication.* Pretty funny, no?)

Laura Purdie Salas
Taking the Plunge: A Teen's Guide to Independence
Sections on finding your own place, budgeting, staying healthy, and more!

Marianne Williamson
A Return to Love
This is one of the greatest books I've ever read. It's about how to live in your heart and not listen to the critical voices that make us crazy and sad.

ACKNOWLEDGEMENTS

Honestly, there isn't a chance in the world that this book would have been written without a lot of support, encouragement, and love. First, let me thank my wonder-husband, Nick: you are the best husband ever. You have sacrificed a lot for me to follow my dreams and I am forever grateful. I love you, honey.

I also want to thank my step kids, Mike and Nichole – for tolerating my weirdness and *always* encouraging me. I couldn't ask for more. I adore you!

To my parents, Jean and Sol: thank you both for your encouraging visits during the writing of this book. Your words gave me strength.

I wouldn't be me without my friends. So to all of my cheerleaders in "The Triangle Club" and in my business & social networks, I would like to say: thank you for your bright smiles, kind words, and good hugs!

Specifically I'd like to thank Amy Lang, a fun, funky, and super generous friend: thanks for believing in my mission. To Deborah Drake, my writing and publishing mentor: thank you for loving my work and sharing your brilliance. To Melissa Wadsworth: thanks for sharing your house and your radiance. You always help me focus on what matters! To Roberta Kuhlman: here's to our loooong friendship and thank you so much for your loving support of my work.

To Daryn: thanks for all your help with the book and all your suggestions. I love you, kiddo, and I'm so proud of you!

And a big hug for my other teen readers: Arden, Caroline, Ethan, Stella, and Nate.

Thanks also to Seattle's Roy Street Café, Holy Grounds Coffeehouse, and Mosaic Coffeehouse for your great atmosphere and friendly staff. I spent many, many hours writing in your comfy chairs!

And, last but not least, to G and the gang: thanks for staying close even when I didn't.

CREDITS

Cover Design:

Seth D. Olson, SEOteks Creative, Graphic Design

Photos:

"Looking Down" © Antonio Jorge Da Silva Nunes | Dreamstime.com
"Couple Problems" © Bidouze Stéphane | Dreamstime.com
"Love of Shoes" © Mehmet Uluç Ceylani | Dreamstime.com
"Margit Crane" © Tara Gimmer Photography

Articles of Interest:

On Mirror Neurons:
pbs.org/wgbh/nova/body/mirror-neurons.html

On Reticular Activation:
xamuel.com/reticular-activation-system/

On the Primitive Brain:
npr.org/templates/story/story.php?storyId=129027124

ABOUT THE AUTHOR

Margit Crane is a step-mom, an ADD/ADHD coach,
and a family-communications expert.
She has THREE Master's Degrees, which she calls her "ADD Ph.D."

A former teacher and school counselor, Margit speaks to students, educators,
and PTAs on ADD/ADHD, family relationships, and success.

To book a presentation for your school or community organization, to
schedule a book talk, or to purchase other books and CDs by Margit Crane,
go to MargitCrane.com

Follow Margit!
on Twitter: @TrainUrParents
on Facebook: @TrainUrParents

Get updates, join the dialogue & learn more about training your parents!